Underwater Home

What Should You Do if You Owe More on Your Home than It's Worth?

Brent T. White

Important Notice:

This book is for informational purposes only and is not intended as legal, financial, tax, or other advice. Each circumstance is different and you should consult with an attorney, accountant, and financial advisor about your individual situation.

For additional information and direction as to where you can get help, visit:

www.brentwhite.com

Table of Contents

Introduction

You probably bought your home thinking that you were making a wise investment and that your home would provide you and your family with stability and financial security in the future. If you now owe more on your home than it's worth, things obviously didn't go as planned. Your home isn't only a bad investment, it may be toxic, and it may be threatening your family's financial future. You may be losing sleep, your marriage may be strained, and you may be paralyzed by anxiety and fear about your future.

You're not alone in feeling worried and unsure what to do. There are as many as 16 million other homeowners who are also "underwater." If you're like many others, your home may have lost much of its value, you may be paying twice what you'd pay to rent, and you may be using up your savings just to stay afloat. If you bought your home as your primary investment for retirement, it may threaten your very ability to retire at all. And, regardless of your precise circumstances, you're almost certainly not getting ahead financially — unlike others before you who have used their home to build a nest egg for the future. Indeed, if you're pouring all your disposable income into your mortgage and not saving for the future, you may be digging yourself into a financial hole out of which you will never fully emerge.

But as distressing as your situation may be, you do have options. First, you can stick it out, which, depending on your circumstances, may be the best financial choice that you can make — even if you're deeply underwater. Second, you can try to arrange a short-sale, which involves selling your house for less than you owe. Third, you can try to get a loan modification to reduce your payments. Fourth, in some circumstances, you may be able to eliminate second and third mortgages for a fraction of the amount owed in Chapter 13 bankruptcy. Fifth, you can stop making payments and voluntarily give up your home to foreclosure.

This book doesn't advocate any particular course of action. It discusses all of your options, so that you can make the best decision for yourself. This book will devote significant time, however, to discussing whether or not you should default on your mortgage. It will do so for two reasons. First, everyone agrees that it's okay for you to keep paying your mortgage. What's controversial is whether or not it's acceptable for you to default and, if so, under what circumstances. Second, and most critically, unless you default on your mortgage, other options such as a loan modification or short-sale are likely off the table for you. Deciding not to default is, in many cases, the equivalent of deciding to do nothing about your situation.

In an ideal world, you wouldn't need to consider default. You would call up your lender, explain your situation, and it would help you out. After all, financial institutions were in large part responsible for the housing collapse. They should step up to the plate and assist underwater homeowners like you. Your lender could, for example, voluntarily reduce your principal balance or at least lower your payments until home prices have recovered. But we don't live in an ideal world and that's not going to happen.

Your lender is in the business of making money. From your lender's perspective, helping you while you're still paying your mortgage is the equivalent of throwing money away. Your lender knows that you'll likely keep making payments even without any help. Though you may feel that you've been a good customer and are deserving of assistance, your lender doesn't see things that way. It's not going to reward you for always making your payments on time. It doesn't care that you've been a loyal customer. To the contrary, your being "responsible" is often the surest way *not* to get help from your lender.

I've heard from many homeowners who can't understand why their lenders won't help them when they've struggled so hard to pay their mortgage on time. Their stories are typically something like these:

> So many of us are upside down in our homes and have no recourse. Unless we deliberately fall behind on our mortgage, there's no help from the mortgage company. So many times, I have called my mortgage company to say that I have been a good paying customer who despite these difficult economic times has continued to pay on time. I am told over and over again that they cannot do anything for me. –N.S.

We have contacted the bank several times to discuss this and they're not interested in negotiating anything different. This is really strange to me because we have excellent credit scores and a good income. But instead of renegotiating the terms of the deal, they will have to do all of the foreclosure paperwork, let the house stand empty, go to the expense of finding a new buyer, sell the house for $200,000 less than we owed to folks who may or may not be as good credit risks as we are. I feel like I have been hit in the stomach. – K.T.

I understand the feeling. Your bank should want to help you out. It would be the compassionate thing to do. But banks are corporations. They don't have feelings, they don't feel empathy, and they're indifferent to your struggle. They exist only to make money. You can save yourself a lot of agony, pain and hurt feelings if you can fully internalize this point. It's just business to your bank. You have to make it just business to you.

If you think like a business, you'll see why your lender isn't likely to give you a loan modification, or agree to a short- sale, as long as you're making your payments. If your lender agrees to either, they're going to lose money. You'll either be paying less on a monthly basis than you're paying right now or they'll have to accept less, as part of a short-sale, than they loaned to you in the first place.

Given these incentives, lenders turn away at the door most underwater homeowners who seek help. Underwater homeowners who are current on their mortgage, and call their lenders for assistance, are almost always told that there is nothing that the lender can do:

> I did speak to my bank but they really have no interest in helping me as long as I continue to make payments. - T. D.

> We've also called the bank to ask for a modification but like many others, because we have always paid on time, they are of no help. - M.I.

> I then attempted a loan modification but the lender would not agree to it unless I was 90 days late on payments. - K. I.

> Because we are not in default with any of the lenders no one is willing to even talk to us about a restructuring program. - S. T.

> My husband and I are underwater and still paying. We have been trying to work out a modification or a refinance with our bank for a year and a half. No success. It was implied that we would need to miss some payments first. - D. L.

I am about to be moved by my employer and Bank of America refuses to negotiate on any level with me because I am current and pay my mortgage on time. -D. S.

Simply put: Your lender isn't likely to work with you if you're current on your mortgage. Your lender has no reason to modify your loan or agree to a short-sale if you're making payments on time. Your lender also knows that the best predictor that you'll continue making payments is a past history of making payments. To your lender, your excellent payment history isn't evidence that you deserve help. It's evidence that you'll go right on paying your mortgage no matter what your bank does.

Moreover, your lender knows that borrowers with good credit scores are unlikely to default even when they're deeply underwater. If you have a good credit score and a solid payment history, your lender isn't likely to be interested in talking with you. You're in a tight spot and your lender knows it. Unfortunately, there's probably only one way out: intentionally defaulting your mortgage.

Your lender is familiar with intentional default, as there's a good chance they've done it themselves at some point in the past. Just last year, for example, Morgan Stanley intentionally defaulted on five buildings in downtown San Francisco. It defaulted on a $2 billion loan and just handed the buildings back to its lender-- even though it made record profits last year and certainly could have paid its mortgage. It just didn't make financial sense to keep paying, so

Morgan Stanley walked away. Morgan Stanley's actions weren't unusual or illegal. Indeed, intentional default is a common practice for corporations and financial institutions when they need to shed a toxic asset, such as an underwater mortgage. What Morgan Stanley and other financial institutions don't want you to know, however, is that you have the same option to default on your mortgage.

Of course, default comes with risks, and these risks are greater in some states than in others. Default also means being willing to lose your house. It's not for everyone. But many underwater homeowners have found a way out of their desperate situations by defaulting on their mortgages. I've heard from hundreds of them, as well as hundreds more underwater homeowners who still feel trapped. Many of these trapped homeowners may be better off if they defaulted as well. This book is designed to give you the information that will enable you to determine if you're one of them.

Default may or may not be the right choice for you. This book will also discuss ways that you can try to get a loan modification without defaulting. Additionally, it will discuss options other than default that may allow you to improve your situation, including using bankruptcy to modify mortgages on rental properties and to eliminate second and third mortgages on your residence for a fraction of the amount owed. This book's purpose is to help you make the best decision for yourself, whatever that decision may be.

To that end, this book will try to cut through the emotions, such as fear, shame and guilt that prevent many underwater homeowners from even considering all their options. It will also empower you to fight the scare and shaming tactics that your lender will likely employ against you:

> So the decision has been made, my last payment was in December. Of course I didn't hear from them until I was 30 days delinquent. When they called to collect, the script was predictable: she threatened my credit would be negatively affected, I would have to repay missed payments with penalties and interest, they would take my home, and I would risk losing other assets. I sensed her frustration when I told her to go ahead and begin the process if they weren't going to restructure. It felt great to take away their leverage! - O.N.

> When I tell them that I have already secured another house to rent...they just sputter and try the moral high ground story. I tell them the house is in very good shape and ready for foreclosure, and to please hurry up and get on with it. That really frustrates them to no end. It's very, very good to have options. –C.D.

Not only is it good to have options, you may end up in a similar situation as Chris Deaner, who appeared with me on "60 Minutes" to talk about his decision to intentionally default on his deeply underwater mortgage. Chris had a credit score of 788 when he first stopped making mortgage payments in January of 2010. He used the money he saved from not paying his mortgage to pay down his other debt. He voluntarily gave up his home to foreclosure in July 2010. By August 2010, his credit score was 743 and he's ecstatic about his financial future:

> I am absolutely thrilled about my future positive net-worth. My wife and I are extremely excited to finally get out from under our lender's chokehold and secure a financially sound future for our family, more importantly our son.

Of course, foreclosure isn't the only possible outcome of default. You may also end up convincing your lender to agree to a loan modification or a short-sale. But if you're ever going to get free from your lender's chokehold, defaulting on your mortgage is usually a necessary first step. Before you can get what you want, you usually have to be willing to walk away.

Chapter 1: The Moral Dimensions

Guilt and Shame

Even if getting out from under your lender's chokehold sounds great, the thought of defaulting on your mortgage might make you uneasy. After all, we've been taught since we were children to honor our commitments, and our mortgage feels like a pretty big one. How could you just stop paying your mortgage? The mere thought of doing so might make you feel guilty. In addition, you may worry about what your neighbors, your friends, or your family would think. These are understandable feelings and you shouldn't do anything that you can't live with in good conscience.

But consider the fact that financial institutions and other powerful interests have acted to make sure that underwater homeowners and not lenders bear the primary burden of the housing collapse. The depressing reality is that our government has chosen to let homeowners suffer under the burden of underwater mortgages rather than force financial institutions to accept responsibility for the housing collapse that they largely caused. Congress could have given courts the power to force banks to reduce the principal on underwater mortgages for struggling homeowners. But banks successfully fought efforts in Congress to give courts this power. The government has chosen to protect the financial health of banks over protecting your financial health. If you and the many underwater homeowners like you default, banks will take big losses. Wall Street doesn't want that. The government doesn't want that. So they want you to keep paying your mortgage.

One way to keep you paying is to cultivate guilt and shame in those who would contemplate walking away. This is done by perpetuating a moral double standard in which it's okay for Morgan Stanley to default, but not for you to do so. The clear message from nearly all fronts is that you have a moral obligation to pay your mortgage. Government officials, including President Obama, have repeatedly emphasized the virtue of homeowners who act "responsibly" and keep "making their mortgage payments each month." Secretary of the Treasury Henry Paulson in the Bush Administration declared: "And let me emphasize, any homeowner who can afford his mortgage payment but chooses to walk away from an underwater property is simply a speculator—and one who isn't honoring his obligations."

Paulson's comment is mild, however, compared to the media attacks on those who default on their mortgages. Individuals who default on their mortgage are frequently portrayed as irresponsible, called deadbeats, and have even been likened to those who would have "given up" and just handed over Europe to the Nazis. None of this inflammatory language is used for corporations like Morgan Stanley that do exactly the same thing.

There's similarly no shortage of moralizing about the responsibilities of underwater homeowners. Typical media messages include: "we need a culture of responsible consumers and homeowners;" "one should always honor financial obligations;" "when you enter into a contract that should mean something;" "there was a time when people felt really

16

bad about not paying off a debt;" and "most people feel, or should feel, an obligation to pay their debts."

Such truisms are repeated over and over in order to make people feel guilty for even contemplating default. But such simplistic statements are based upon a complete lack of understanding of what it means — or how it feels — to be underwater on your mortgage. People don't typically default on their mortgages because they don't value their commitments. As the following examples illustrate, they default because they're overwhelmed by the stress and anxiety of being underwater on their mortgage and because they have to make tough, painful choices about what to do:

> I am a single mother and have been saddled with a home that I just can't afford. I have done everything to hold on to avoid the shame of foreclosure.... I have racked up over twenty thousand dollars in debt trying to keep things afloat, hoping I could eventually sell the home and pay off my credit debt - and break even. What a foolish thing for me to do. The house is appraising less and less every year- and nothing is moving in the neighborhood.... I was advised to allow the house to go into foreclosure - which I have reluctantly begun to do (I have never missed or been late on any payment ever). - N. L.

We're not proud of our circumstances. We always had excellent credit and have honored our financial obligations on all of our other homes, cars and credit card companies. But this is what we must do, as scary as it is. - L. B.

We did not default without numerous conversations, discussions, and soul searching beyond belief. The hardest part to justify is the loss we may have caused our neighbors. They weren't paying our bills though. - Q. B.

Far from not worrying enough about their commitments, I think many underwater homeowners worry too much. As you know if you're struggling under your mortgage, being underwater can create a great deal of anxiety, stress, and internal conflict. It can also be very lonely, isolating and psychologically challenging to sort things out in your mind. Too many homeowners suffer in silence. They also heap themselves with self-recrimination, even though they couldn't have predicted and didn't cause the housing meltdown.

If you're like others, you may blame yourself for not seeing this coming. If you hadn't been in such a rush to buy a home; if you had listened to that voice inside telling you that home prices seemed crazy; if you hadn't put all your eggs in the homeownership basket; and--better yet—if you had just rented instead, you wouldn't find yourself in this mess.

But hindsight is 20-20. You weren't being

foolish or reckless *at the time* to buy a house. To the contrary, experts were telling you that buying a home was the wisest thing that you could do. In 2004, for example, experts at the financial magazine *Forbes* claimed, "Home ownership rewards most buyers and, barring a severe economic downturn, it's as close as it gets to a 'can't miss' investment." Similarly, the Secretary of Housing and Urban Development Alphonso Jackson proclaimed in 2007 that "owning a home remains the best long-term investment a family can make."

Likewise, the National Association of Realtors® (NAR) launched a $40 million campaign in 2006 as the housing market began to crash to convince you that it was a "great time to buy." In July 2006, for example, the NAR released a "consumer education brochure" called *"To Buy Or Not To Buy?"* This brochure misleadingly claimed that, "[r]enting can cost more than seven times annually than owning," when in actuality price-to-rent ratios were so out of line in many markets that it cost two to three times a month more to own than to rent. Nevertheless, in a message to its agent members, the NAR implored: "Are your clients still on the fence about buying a home? Then tell them what they need to know! Homeownership is easier and less expensive than renting."

Not only was owning less expensive, the brochure claimed, it was also a safe investment and an effective way to build wealth: "The Federal Reserve Board estimates the homeowners have a net worth nearly 36 times more than that of renters." The brochure also suggested that steady appreciation of at

19

least 4.5% was pretty much in the bag:

> For the majority of Americans, their home is their largest financial asset and a major player in their investment portfolio. It's a good thing, too. The NATIONAL ASSOCIATION OF REALTORS® estimates that home value rises, on average, by 4.5 percent a year. That's a steady return on investment; one's own home is a much less volatile asset than stocks, bonds, or mutual funds.

NAR's *Realtor Magazine* also provided scripts for agents to repeat to their buying clients. If your agent was following one of these scripts, they may have told you that real estate prices might "stabilize," but would never go down, and that you'd better jump before you missed your "window of opportunity." If you expressed any concern about the housing market, your agent may have repeated a NAR script designed to assure you that "all real estate is local," that your market was strong, and that you were making a wise and safe investment.

It's not your fault if you believed this message. You were hearing it from all quarters. You're not morally obligated to suffer the rest of your life for making the mistake of believing what you were being told by the so-called experts.

Nevertheless, the near-uniform message promoted by the financial industry and their allies is that defaulting on your mortgage is wrong. Indeed, even many "non-profit" credit-counseling agencies promote this message. For example, Gail Cunningham of the National Foundation for Credit Counseling declared in an interview on National Public Radio (NPR) that, "Walking away from one's home should be the absolute last resort. However desperate a situation might become for a homeowner, that does not relieve us of our responsibilities." Ms. Cunningham does not reveal on NPR that the National Foundation for Credit Counseling is funded in part by the credit industry. It's not surprising that she thinks you should pay your mortgage.

Similarly, Fannie Mae answers the question, "Is it best to walk away from my property if I can no longer make the payments?" as follows: "Walking away from your property isn't a good choice." That's what you should expect from Fannie Mae as the nation's largest U.S. mortgage-finance company. Fannie Mae, in turn, is owned by the federal government. So you can see the government's self-interest in telling you that you have a moral obligation to pay your mortgage as well.

But what makes the message of personal responsibility so effective is that it's not just Fannie Mae and the government. The financial industry, the media, and "non-profits" all tend to speak with one voice. Thus, when the government or the credit industry tells you that you have an obligation to pay your mortgage, even if you're desperate and seriously underwater, the message seems to echo a common social consensus. As such, you aren't likely to perceive the message as an effort to saddle you with the primary burden of the housing meltdown rather than the financial industry. The message of responsibility probably rings true to your ear. As such, you're not likely to question its content or source. Let's take a step back though and see if the message holds up to examination.

Mortgages are Just Contracts

The moral argument against defaulting on your mortgage generally boils down to the same three basic points. First, you "promised" to pay your mortgage when you signed the mortgage contract, and it would be immoral for you to break this promise. Second, foreclosures lead to depreciation of neighborhoods, so you should hang on in order to help preserve your neighbors' property values. And, third, if all underwater homeowners defaulted, the housing market might crash. You thus have a social obligation to pay your mortgage in order to save the economy.

Let's take these arguments in order. First, a mortgage contract, like all other contracts, is purely a legal document, not a moral promise. Think of it this way: when you got your cell phone, you likely signed a contract with your carrier in which you "promised" to pay a set monthly payment for two years. Let's say, though, that two months after you sign your contract, the price of cell phone service drops by half--meaning that the same cell phone service for which you pay $100 a month can be had for half that with another carrier. You decide that you would be financially better off paying the early termination fee of $300 rather than $100 a month for another 22 months for the same service that you can now get for $50.

Would it be immoral for you to break your contractual "promise" to pay $100 for two years, and elect instead to pay the early termination fee? Of course not. The option to break your "promise" to pay is part of the contract, as is the consequence — a $300 early termination fee. There's absolutely nothing immoral about your breaking your "promise," and you'd be financially wise to do so. Though a mortgage contract is more substantial, the principle is the same. Like a cell phone contract, a mortgage contract explicitly sets out the consequences of breaking the promise to pay.

In other words, your lender contemplated in advance that you might be unable or unwilling to continue making payments on your mortgage at some point, and decided in advance what fair compensation to the lender would be. The lender then wrote that compensation into the contract. Specifically, your lender probably included clauses in your contract providing that it may foreclose on your property, keep any payments that you have made, and may opt to pursue a deficiency judgment against you, if state law so allows. A deficiency judgment is a court order to pay the lender's losses as a result of a foreclosure sale. In other words, it's an order to pay the difference between what you owe and what the lender was able to get for your house at foreclosure.

As we will discuss later, even in states where they can, lenders frequently don't pursue borrowers for deficiency judgments, because it's often not economically worthwhile to do so. Nevertheless, that's the agreement. By writing this consequence into the contract, your lender agreed to accept your property and (in most states) the *option* to pursue a deficiency judgment against you in lieu of payment. No one forced your lender to sign — or write — that contract. And, to be sure, your lender wouldn't hesitate to exercise its right to take your house if it was in its financial interest to do so. Concerns of morality or social responsibility wouldn't be part of the equation. Indeed, banks are generally eager to foreclose on homes with significant positive equity, even if the homeowner has simply fallen on hard times after responsibly paying the mortgage for years. Your bank just doesn't want *your* house because you're underwater.

The attitude of banks is exemplified by the CEO of JP Morgan Chase, who testified before Congress that modifying principal balances on underwater mortgages in order to stem foreclosures would be "irresponsible" because modification isn't contemplated in the mortgage contract. In other words, banks only care about what's in the contract.

That's a good thing for you, because your contract contains an option to default. Indeed, by JP Morgan Chase's logic, it would be "irresponsible" for you not to exercise it. Your bank understands that the mortgage contract imposes no moral or social responsibilities on it and behaves accordingly. Why shouldn't you?

If you default, your contract provides that you just have to be willing to accept the consequences contained in the contract. But there's no moral responsibility clause in your contract. And, if there was, it wouldn't be legally enforceable. As far as the law is concerned, defaulting is no more immoral than choosing to cancel a cell phone contract. Your lender would feel free to do it if it were in your shoes.

Moreover, your lender knew the bargain that it

was making when it loaned you the money, including that it was loaning money on a home with a possibly inflated price. It also knew that you might default if prices crashed. Indeed, your lender factored that risk into the price of the loan and made you pay for it as part of the interest rate. Additionally, if you live in a state like Arizona or California where you can default on most purchase money mortgages without a risk of a deficiency judgment, you paid on average an additional $800 at closing per $100,000 borrowed for the option to default without being on the hook for your mortgage balance. It's like an insurance policy. You paid for an option to default, and there's nothing immoral about your exercising it.

If your lender miscalculated the risk of defaults due to a housing collapse, that's not your fault. You aren't barred from collecting on an insurance policy if your insurance company miscalculates the chances of a tornado and wishes that they had charged you more. If your lender miscalculated the risk of a housing collapse and borrowers defaulting as a result, that's the lender's error. It will be more careful next time. But you still have an option to default. As Nobel Prize winning economist Joseph Stiglitz has explained, "[F]or the most part, the lenders were, or should have been, far more financially sophisticated than the borrowers." Lenders "should be made to bear the consequences of their failures to assess risk."

Lenders should also bear the consequences of their failure to ensure that the collateral for the mortgage was worth what they loaned. A textbook premise of economics is that a home's value is "the current value of the rent payments that could be

earned from renting the property at market prices."
As such, historically home prices have hewed
nationally to a price-to-rent ratio of roughly 15:1. At
the peak of the market, however, national price-to-
rent ratios reached 23:1, and 50:1 in the most inflated
markets. Lenders were surely aware of this fact, but
chose to ignore the risk.

You, on the other hand, may have thought that
the lender wouldn't have loaned you the money if the
house wasn't worth that much. You also may have
relied upon the results of the appraisal arranged by
the lender as some assurance that you were paying a
fair price for your house. Little did you know that
your lender may not have cared if the house was
really worth the value of the loan, because it intended
to sell the loan to someone else for a quick profit.
Indeed, unbeknownst to you, your mortgage broker
may have "suggested" a price to the appraiser to
insure that your house appraised for at least the
purchase price. Once the appraisal appeared to
support the purchase price, they could issue the loan,
make a nice profit, and leave you holding the bag.

Moreover, given that your lender wrote and
surely understood the mortgage contract that it
signed with you, it's not unfair to hold your lender to
its agreement. Your lender agreed that it would
accept the option of foreclosing on your home and, in
some states, the right to pursue a deficiency judgment
if you defaulted. Because lenders know that default is
possible in any mortgage contract, careful lenders
ensure that they won't lose money in the event of
default and foreclosure. In other words, careful
lenders make sure that the house is worth at least as

much as the loan, and that the borrower has made a big enough down payment to have some skin in the game. Lenders who didn't do these things during the housing bubble assumed the risk that borrowers would default if there was a housing meltdown. They have no one to blame but themselves for not being more careful in their lending practices. It's ironic, though, how banks only like to talk about personal responsibility in reference to homeowners.

Keeping Promises

Despite the fact that your lender assumed the risk of default, and even though the law doesn't treat default as a moral wrong, you may still feel that you should keep your promises. That's a fine belief. Indeed, I hold the same belief. But why treat the promise to pay your mortgage as any more unbreakable than any other promise? If you stop and think about it, you can probably come up with many examples from your life when you had to break a promise. And you probably did so without considering yourself immoral. I recently promised my daughter, for example, that I'd pick her up early from preschool. Though I take promises to my children very seriously, I had to break this one because of a crisis at work. I had competing obligations and had to make a choice. Though some may quibble with my choice, it wasn't immoral. Even my four-year-old daughter understood.

In short, it's simplistic to suggest, as some do, that it's always immoral to break a promise. A more accurate description of the norm is that we should keep our promises unless we have a compelling enough reason not to. For example, needing to move in order to take care of a seriously ill family member would be a good reason—at least in most people's estimation—for a renter to break a lease agreement. The renter would still have to face the risk that some unforgiving landlord may pursue him for the remainder of the lease payments, but few would think the renter immoral for taking that risk. Indeed, not only is breaking a promise frequently acceptable; sometimes it's the most moral thing to do.

This is no less true for a mortgage contract. If you're like many Americans, your home is probably your primary investment. With encouragement from the government, the financial sector, and the real estate industry, you probably saw investing in your home as a route to retirement security, or as a means through accumulated equity of sending your children to college. Given what you were told by the so-called experts, this was a perfectly reasonable hope at the time. But this hope may have vanished for you with the housing collapse. Moreover, because housing prices were so high during the boom, you may have been forced to stretch to buy even a modest home, meaning that all or most of your disposable income now goes to your mortgage, with little left for savings.

You may have understood at the time that you were stretching to buy a home. Indeed, you may have had no choice if you wanted to buy a house because prices were so high. But you may have decided that putting all your money into your mortgage would be like forced savings. Through no fault of your own, things didn't go as planned. As a result of the housing collapse, you may now find yourself pouring all or most of your disposable income into a home that is no longer an investment, but rather a toxic threat to your family's financial security.

If you're like many other underwater homeowners, you may be faced with a choice between paying your mortgage or satisfying some other important financial need. If you've lost your job, paying the mortgage may mean cleaning out your bank accounts and using up your savings. Indeed, many homeowners who have written to me unfortunately don't even consider default until they have greatly depleted or exhausted their reserves:

> My husband and I were laid off almost a year ago now. We're up to date on our mortgage payments and bills but our savings are now gone along with most of our retirement account that we cashed in to keep afloat. We're upside down on our home and have a second mortgage so selling isn't an option. I looked into a Short Sale but I don't think we can keep up with the payments for the months it would take for that to go through...if it would at all. We're considering just walking away from our home or filing bankruptcy. -K.S.

Even if you're not unemployed, paying the mortgage may threaten your retirement security, or your ability to retire at all. If you're in this situation, you—like many homeowners— probably bought your home as part of your investment strategy for retirement:

> We bought our house with the expectation that it would be a fair investment and we could at least break even in about 10 years when we retire.

At this point, we won't be able to retire until our late 80s. – K.T.

We struggle over what to do, at 50 years old we can't continue to throw away what little money we have in this house. - Q. T.

I live in Chicago-area, have a nasty loan from Countrywide and now find myself owing $320,000 more than what the house is currently worth. We're in our late forties...we can keep the house if we pay on an interest-only until we're 80. -K. E.

If not threatening your retirement, continuing to pay your mortgage may create tensions with your obligation to provide for your children's future, including paying for their college:

Not to mention that I have two daughters in college whose education we're funding mainly with loans because we have not been able to save or have any extra funds to assist them in obtaining an education. –N.S.

If you're among the most financially stretched, you may be faced with the choice of defaulting on your mortgage or having to use credit cards to stay afloat:

We have drained out our savings paying our mortgage because of the fear of being late. I just made November's payment on the 30th and don't know how we're going to pay December. Our mortgage servicer offers no extensions. We've spent everything we have to keep our credit intact. We do have a Discover card with a $9,000 limit and no balance but really don't want to put ourselves in more of a hole. We could use the blank checks from it to pay the mortgage and hope I find the job I deserve and have the funds to pay it back, but I know it's unwise to pay for an interest bearing debt with funds from another. It sounds so beneficial to save a couple hundred dollars a month right now, that's money for food, gas, clothing and so on. At which point in time does it become OK to stop paying the mortgage? - O.N.

I'll tell you what I think. I think it's ok to stop paying the mortgage long before you clean out your savings, sacrifice your retirement, spend your children's college fund, and certainly before you have to start using your credit cards to survive. Before you do any of those things, I think the more moral course is to *stop* paying your mortgage. Indeed, I think it's morally acceptable to default if your mortgage threatens your ability to save adequately for the future, regardless of whether you can pay it according to some arbitrary definition of "affordability." It may be more responsible to put the money saved from giving up your home and renting instead into an investment account, so that you are secure in retirement. Or put it into a college fund, so that you can give your children a chance at a higher education.

In other words, things aren't so black-and-white. Given the unprecedented nature of the housing collapse, it should at least be possible for reasonable people to disagree about the most moral or responsible course of action for underwater homeowners. *No one is entitled to sit in judgment of you.*

Your "promise" to pay the mortgage, such as it is, may need to give way to more important obligations — especially since the lender specifically contemplated the possibility of your defaulting in the mortgage contract and willingly assumed that risk. As one underwater homeowner who wrote to me explained, "With a baby boy on the way, it's our duty to make financially sound decisions in this upcoming year and plan to be very savvy on our future endeavors as well." Or, as another said, "we have two little boys ages 10 and 12 and we must think about their futures." I applaud these homeowners for deciding for themselves where their main responsibilities lie.

Obligations to Society and Neighbors

Your mortgage contract is between you and your lender. Yet it's commonly argued that defaulting on your mortgage is socially irresponsible, because foreclosures hurt neighborhoods and the overall economy. This can be a powerful argument because most homeowners don't want to feel like they're hurting others by their actions. And they certainly don't want to be responsible for causing their neighbors to suffer. This is a good thing. It's right to be concerned about others.

But it's a lot to ask of you or any other homeowner to prop up neighborhood property values on your back. It's especially a lot to ask if it means squandering your savings, foregoing retirement, raiding your children's college fund, or using your credit cards to buy groceries.

Moreover, concern for others goes both ways. It wouldn't be fair for your neighbor to want you to suffer financially — perhaps for the rest of your life — so that their house may or may not be temporarily more valuable on paper. Though your neighbors' concerns for their property values are understandable, it would be selfish of them to want you to sacrifice your family's financial future so that they could feel better about their net worth.

Additionally, your defaulting on your mortgage will likely have very little long-term effect on home prices in your neighborhood, and less still on the economy as a whole. Indeed, according to the National Consumer Law Center, one foreclosure reduces home prices within a neighborhood less than 1%. Moreover, if houses in your neighborhood are overpriced, they are likely to come down no matter what you do. Then you're going to be even more underwater. On the other hand, if home prices in your neighborhood are where they should be, but take a slight dip because your house sells at a discount, they will come back up. Home prices will go up or down according to forces that are completely outside your control. You couldn't prop up home values in your neighborhood even if you tried, and you can't single-handedly destroy them, either. Whether or not you default isn't likely to have any long-term effect on your neighbor, but it may make all the difference to your financial future.

Additionally, the notion that it would be bad for the economy if more people defaulted is contested by many economists, though it's often repeated as if it were biblical truth by the media. A number of well-regarded economists argue that it would actually be beneficial for the economy and the housing market if more people defaulted. These economists point out that there are economic benefits to society when people shed their underwater mortgages. First, being underwater reduces consumer spending. This is called the negative wealth effect. Whereas people who have lots of equity in their homes feel wealthy and thus spend more money, people who are underwater feel poor, so they spend little. You probably understand this phenomenon from first-hand experience.

The more people there are like you who are underwater on their mortgages, the weaker consumer spending is in the overall economy. This could, in fact, be a part of why the economy has been so slow to recover. Just think about what it means to an average family to be tens of thousands of dollars underwater on their mortgage; then multiply this times 16 million homeowners. It's easy to see why this isn't a good thing for the economy. If more people defaulted, however, and thus fewer people were underwater on their mortgages, it might mean more consumer spending. In that sense, more defaults might be *good* for the economy.

Second, if you're unemployed or underemployed, but can't move to take a new job elsewhere because you're underwater on your mortgage, this is a really bad thing for the economy. An efficient national economy is one with a mobile labor market where individuals are able to move to take new jobs. Worker mobility is a key to our national economy because we need people to be able to move where the jobs are and for people to do the job that makes the best use of their talents. The fact that people can't move to take new jobs because they're underwater has a range of negative effects on the economy, including increased structural unemployment and reduced productivity. Indeed, a report by the International Monetary Fund recently found that lack of mobility due to underwater mortgages is part of the reason for current, persistent high unemployment in the United States.

To put this in plain English, you aren't doing yourself or the rest of us any favor by foregoing a good job opportunity elsewhere because you'd have to walk away from your underwater home. Go ahead. Take the job if you want it. If you have to walk away or list your house as a short-sale, someone will be lucky to buy your home at a good price, society will benefit from your talents being utilized instead of wasted, and your family will benefit from your being able to put food on the table.

The story that the economy will crash if people walk away from their mortgages is the story that Wall Street wants everyone to believe. It's a variant, in fact, of the story that was used to hoist the bailout of financial institutions upon us during the financial meltdown. We've been conditioned to believe that the financial health of Main Street depends upon the health of Wall Street. If financial institutions suffer losses, we're told that we're going to suffer too. This was enough to scare the public into acceding to the taxpayer bailout of Wall Street; and it's enough to scare people into thinking that we need to do everything we can to keep people from defaulting on their mortgages, including verbally attacking our struggling neighbors who decide to default. Better to turn neighbor against neighbor than to require Wall Street to take losses.

What's really at issue is who bears the primary burden of the housing collapse, financial institutions or underwater homeowners. You shouldn't just accept the story that preventing people from defaulting on their mortgages is about saving the economy. The main players advancing this theory are allied with financial institutions, which are primarily concerned with protecting themselves from losses. Moreover, all this talk about the economy collapsing if homeowners default obscures one simple point:

people wouldn't have to default if banks were willing to voluntarily modify mortgages. It boils down to a question of fairness. Who should have to bear the burden of the housing collapse? You or your bank? You may be willing to share the burden with your bank, but your bank wants it all on you.

Underwater homeowners who keep making their payments have received little help, even though the only mistake that most made was to buy a house at the wrong time. Major banks, on the other hand, were bailed out for grossly irresponsible behavior. Many of them are now, as a result, raking in billions of dollars in profits again. Yet they have still largely refused to help underwater homeowners by voluntarily modifying mortgages — despite the great benefits doing so would provide for the homeowner, the economy, and society. Banks, which were shown great mercy in the bailout, have shown little mercy for underwater homeowners.

In their singular focus on maximizing profits, financial institutions have also taken little responsibility for preventing the destruction of neighborhoods. Not only have they resisted efforts to stem foreclosures, banks sometimes abandon the very houses that they foreclose upon--leaving them to fall into disrepair and neglect, and to be taken over by weeds and graffiti. This kind of behavior destroys neighborhoods, and requires cities to raze whole city blocks.

Though financial institutions bear primary responsibility for causing this crisis, the behavior of many banks in the wake of the crisis has been nothing less than unconscionable. Given this fact, it's remarkable that so much condemnation has been directed at struggling underwater homeowners who decide to abandon a sinking ship instead of the banks who refuse to throw them a lifeline.

The Moral Double Standard

Not only have homeowners and not financial institutions been called to sacrifice their own well-being for the common good, financial institutions are rarely criticized when they default on their own mortgages. Intentional default is a common practice among financial institutions and large corporations. For example, in early 2010, in the biggest real estate default in history, real estate giant Tishman Speyer Properties intentionally defaulted on $4.4 billion in loans on Stuyvesant Town and Peter Cooper Village in New York City, after the properties lost $2 billion in value. Tishman Speyer did this despite having billions of dollars in assets, including Manhattan's Rockefeller Center and the Chrysler Building, that it could have leveraged or sold to meet its obligations under the loans.

Similarly, as previously discussed, Morgan Stanley walked away from a $2 billion mortgage on five buildings in San Francisco last year, despite raking in record profits. Morgan Stanley officials stated, "This isn't a default or foreclosure situation. We're going to give them the properties to get out of the loan obligation." Sure sounds like a default to me, and indeed it was. But such behavior hasn't dented Morgan Stanley's reputation on Wall Street. Yet try calling your lender and seeing how it responds if you say that you'd like do what Morgan Stanley did and give your lender your property to get out of your loan obligation. They'll say no and probably hang up the phone. Indeed, Morgan Stanley, which holds the mortgages of thousands of Americans, hasn't been nearly as forgiving to homeowners as it was to itself.

Similarly, the Mortgage Bankers Association forced a short-sale on a $70 million mortgage when the association's building in Washington, DC lost half its value. It has subsequently refused to answer any questions about whether it defaulted on its mortgage or will pay the deficiency. This is the same Mortgage Bankers Association, by the way, who's CEO, Jon Carlson, said of homeowners who default: "What about the message they will send to their family and their kids and their friends by defaulting?" That's not only a double standard, that's hypocrisy. Underwater homeowners are told that they should sell everything that they have and cash out their retirement plan to pay the mortgage, while corporations and the Mortgage Bankers Association are able to "get out of their loan obligations."

Some commentators have attempted to justify this double talk by arguing that commercial mortgage contracts are somehow fundamentally different from residential mortgage contracts. These commentators suggest that parties to commercial mortgage contracts contemplate the possibility of default in advance and agree on the remedy – typically, surrender of the property. They argue that parties to residential mortgages, on the other hand, contemplate only that the mortgage will be repaid. Thus, it is argued, residential mortgage contracts contain an implicit promise to pay regardless of market conditions that is absent from commercial mortgage contracts.

This argument has no legal basis and depends on the public's ignorance of contract law. Residential mortgage contracts, just like commercial mortgage contracts, contemplate the possibility of default and contain an agreed-upon remedy. It's true that sophisticated and powerful corporations frequently negotiate more favorable terms for themselves than the average homeowner. But this isn't a moral difference, and it doesn't change the fact that both types of contracts contain agreed-upon remedies in the event of default. Indeed, given the power imbalance between residential borrowers and banks, society should be more forgiving of individual homeowners than corporations.

But whether society is less forgiving or not, it just can't be the case that it's morally acceptable for financial institutions and large corporations to default on their mortgages, as long as they're willing to bear the contractually-agreed-upon consequence, but it's not okay for you to do exactly the same thing. There shouldn't be two sets of rules in America.

Indeed, the Supreme Court recently held that corporations – with all their wealth and power - have the same free speech rights that you do. Because of this, they can now spend as much money as they want to influence elections and make sure that their interests are protected in Washington. This further decreases the chance that Congress will ever act to help underwater homeowners. But why shouldn't equal rights go both ways? If wealthy corporations have the same rights to free speech as you, why shouldn't you have the same right to look out for your financial best interest?

Chapter 2: Practical Worries

Anxiety about Foreclosure

In addition to trying to make you feel guilty, the main way that your lender, the government, and others keep you in your underwater home is to scare you into thinking that foreclosure is the end of the world. Here are a few examples of the exaggerated claims that you may have heard about foreclosure (only read them if you can do so without taking them too seriously):

> What is real—and what is very much downplayed...is how completely a foreclosure wrecks your finances. Near term, you might get slammed with a massive tax bill, since forgiven debt can be subject to income tax. Long term, car loans and—you guessed it—home loans will be much harder to come by. How's that for walking away? - *Time Magazine*.

> The thing that homeowners have to take into consideration here is that this is a real disaster for your credit, if you have a foreclosure on your record, even default. But if you fall behind on your mortgage, and don't pay it, everyone you go to borrow money from for the next six or seven years is going to know about this. When you try to go for a job, when you try to rent an apartment, this is going to be on your credit. It's not

like you walk away scot-free, you walk away with a huge black mark on your credit rating. - *Nightline, 2008*

Losing your home can be the worst and most devastating event to you personally, and your credit history. This is a scenario that you don't want to occur if you can avoid it! Not only will you lose the comfort of your home and your investment, but a foreclosure will stay pending on your credit history for as long as 10 years. This will jeopardize your ability to qualify for any future home loan purchases, it may affect your ability to access loans for car purchases and other needed purchases, and loan costs are likely to be higher both in fees and interest paid. - *Anaheim Housing Counseling Agency*

That's scary stuff for sure. It's intended to be. But contrast those doomsday scenarios to what people have to say who have actually gone through foreclosure after intentionally defaulting:

Choosing to walk away was the hardest thing I think I've ever battled with. After walking away, I have felt nothing but relief. –E.G.

My house went into foreclosure sale on July 6 and sold for about $120k loss for about $126k…The foreclosure sale has now been reported and my score as of today is 743 (excellent) up 42 pts from June and down only 45 pts from my original score. It looks like the credit score scare from foreclosing was all a bunch of media hype….Not to mention I have positive net worth now. -CD

I applied for a loan modification two months after I stopped paying. Fortunately with not paying the mortgage I have been able to afford to pay my other bills down, and pay off monthly my one remaining credit card with its $1000 limit. Interestingly, my credit score has already recovered to 650. Who needs/wants credit anyway?! That is what got us all into trouble. – L.R.

The foreclosure proceedings are now officially behind us and it was as you said a relatively painless process. – R.S.

Why the discrepancy between what the "experts" say and the real-life experiences of those who choose voluntary foreclosure? Much of it is scare tactics, pure and simple. For example, despite the warnings above, if you default on a loan used to purchase or improve your primary residence, you aren't going to get slammed with a massive tax bill, because the Mortgage Debt Forgiveness Act provides that forgiven debt on such mortgages isn't currently subject to income tax. Also, absent some mistake, a foreclosure isn't going to stay on your credit record for ten years; it's going to stay on for seven. Moreover, the effect of the foreclosure will essentially disappear within three years. So, don't just accept everything that you hear about the dire consequences of foreclosure.

Sure, your credit's going to take a temporary hit and it might be a big one. Some credit cards may cancel or lower your credit limits. But you'll recover. You'll likely do so much sooner than you would have thought. If your credit score is already low, defaulting on your mortgage may actually help you *improve* your credit score.

More on credit scores and taxes later. For now, the important thing to know about a foreclosure is that you can plan for it. First, you can get your life in order before you default. I've taken a lot of heat from the banking industry and its allies for suggesting in an earlier article that one who plans to default can take steps to minimize its costs. For example, I suggest that underwater homeowners could purchase a vehicle or other necessities before beginning the process of defaulting. I also suggest that "most individuals should be able to plan in advance for a few years of limited credit."

I fail to see what's so outrageous about that suggestion. If a winter storm is coming, we go to the store to buy milk, bread, and maybe some salt for the driveway. If a hurricane is coming, we board up the house. And if you're going to be without access to easy credit for a while, you should store up on the things you might need to buy on credit during that time. As long as you make these new purchases with the full intent to pay for them, there's nothing legally or morally wrong with your doing so. To the contrary, it's what a prudent person would do.

Second, once you stop paying your mortgage, you'll typically have 4-6 months (and maybe many more) to live mortgage-payment-free in your house before you have to leave. There's nothing wrong with this. It's preferable to abandoning the house and letting it fall into disrepair. And it's better for your neighbors and the lender if you stay and keep the house in good shape. As a bonus, during that time, you can the save the money that you would have paid for your mortgage, or pay down your other debt. If you do that, default can be part of a debt-free-living plan. And debt-free living can be wonderful indeed.

Third, you can prepare to move out in an orderly fashion, take your time packing, and be out before the foreclosure is complete. Once you know the laws in your state, you can figure out the date that you need to leave, mark it on your calendar, and start preparing. In many ways, foreclosure can be more orderly than selling your house, because with selling you never quite know when, or if, you are going to get an offer and have to move out.

Fear of Being Pursued by Your Lender

The primary risk that you face if you default on your mortgage, and can't work out a short-sale, is that your lender may pursue a deficiency judgment against you. A deficiency judgment is a court order that requires you to repay the bank for any money that it lost on the foreclosure. In other words, if you owe $150,000, but your house sells for $100,000, you could theoretically be subject to a deficiency judgment of $50,000, plus costs. That's scary. But like all the other costs of default, the actual risk of such a judgment is frequently exaggerated by the banking industry and its spokespersons precisely because it *is* scary. Scaring you is a good way to make you pay your mortgage.

What's more, guilt and fear are a potent combination. Most of us have a deep-seated belief that if we do "bad things," bad things will happen to us. Most of us simply don't believe that we will escape punishment for our "sins." Guilt and fear of punishment go together. So, if you believe that defaulting on your mortgage is immoral, the notion that you will suffer great consequences for doing so not only seems possible, but feels quite right: it just can't be possible that you can default on your mortgage with no significant consequence. As such, you may not question apocalyptic descriptions of the consequences of defaulting on your mortgage. But let's look at the facts.

First, and very importantly, foreclosure isn't the only possible outcome of default. Lenders are increasingly favoring short-sales over foreclosure, meaning that you may have a chance of convincing your lender to agree to a short-sale. There's also an outside chance that you may be able to work out a loan modification. And, if neither of those work, the lender may be willing to accept a deed-in-lieu of foreclosure, which means foregoing the foreclosure if you'll just sign over the deed. Sometimes the lender will even pay you to do so. This is called *"cash for keys."* Nevertheless, if you default, foreclosure is a likely outcome – so the risk of being pursued for a deficiency judgment has to be part of your calculation in deciding to default.

The risk may be less than you think. In some states, banks may not pursue you for a deficiency judgment on most purchase money mortgages; some particular types of loans carry little risk of a deficiency judgment no matter the state; and, even in states where lenders can pursue deficiency judgments without restriction, they usually don't. If they do, the deficiency judgment can frequently be discharged in bankruptcy.

The following states prohibit deficiency judgments for <u>most</u> *residential, purchase money mortgages*:

- Alaska
- Arizona
- California
- Minnesota
- Montana
- Nevada (but only for mortgages after October 1, 2009)
- North Carolina

- North Dakota
- Oklahoma
- Oregon
- Washington

Some of these states, such as California and Arizona, extend this protection to certain non-purchase money mortgages in certain circumstances. But don't just assume if you live in one of these states that you're in the clear. There are exceptions to the general rule. If you live in any of these states, you should talk to an attorney who can review your particular loan and let you know if you're safe from a deficiency judgment. You may very well be.

Moreover, even if your state isn't on this list, a number of states limit your lender's right to pursue a deficiency judgment in other significant ways. For example, Connecticut, Georgia, Idaho, Nebraska, New Jersey, Oklahoma, and Utah require lenders to pursue a deficiency judgment within three months of foreclosure or else they're barred from doing so. In New Mexico, lenders generally can't pursue deficiency judgments against individuals who make less than 80% of the state's median income. In other states, lenders are barred from collecting a deficiency unless they can prove in a separate proceeding that the foreclosure sale was "commercially reasonable" and that they paid a "fair price" if they bought it themselves. Many, if not most, lenders don't bother with the hassle.

Only Alabama, Delaware, the District of Columbia, Illinois, Indiana, Kentucky, Maryland, Massachusetts, Mississippi, Missouri, Virginia, and

Wyoming allow lenders to pursue deficiencies against foreclosed homeowners without any significant restrictions.

Even if you live in a state that allows deficiency judgments, certain mortgages are essentially non-recourse regardless of the state. For example, the FHA as a matter of present policy does not pursue homeowners for deficiency judgments after foreclosure if the borrower is facing hardship and cooperates in a short-sale, which the FHA calls a pre-foreclosure sale process (PFS). FHA policy states:

> If a foreclosure occurs after the mortgagor unsuccessfully participated in the PFS process in good faith, neither the mortgagee nor HUD will pursue the mortgagor for a deficiency judgment.

Similar rules apply to VA loans. In addition, lenders are required with FHA and VA loans to consider options other than foreclosure, such as short-sales and loan modifications, as long as you can show hardship. But they can't help you until you're at imminent risk of default and usually won't help you unless you actually default.

Moreover, it's the general practice of many lenders, including Fannie Mae, to buy foreclosed homes themselves at foreclosure sales for the outstanding balance, plus fees and costs. Most state laws provide that if lenders do this, there's no deficiency to collect because the house would have sold for the amount owed. As such, many mortgages in the United States carry no practical risk of a deficiency judgment.

Many states also require lenders to go through an onerous and time-consuming judicial foreclosure process if they want to pursue a deficiency judgment. Some of these states give lenders the option to do a "non-judicial foreclosure," which is much cheaper and faster than a judicial foreclosure, if they give up the right to pursue a deficiency judgment. When given this choice, lenders usually prefer "non-judicial foreclosure" and waive the right to pursue a deficiency judgment. If they pursue "non-judicial foreclosure" in such states, you're safe.

If you'd like to know the rules in your state, you can find a *50 State Survey of Foreclosure Laws*, as well as other information, on the National Consumer Law Center website at: http://www.nclc.org/issues/state-foreclosure-laws.html. You can also find information about foreclosure laws on the website for Realtytrac, which has a user-friendly chart of *Foreclosure Laws and Procedures by State*, with separate pages for each state with a nice summary of each state's foreclosure laws, at: http://www.realtytrac.com/foreclosure-laws/foreclosure-laws-comparison.asp

Because foreclosure rules can be complicated and are subject to change, however, you should confirm this information and discuss your particular situation with an attorney before defaulting on your mortgage. *Indeed, before you any make a final decision about what to do about your underwater mortgage, you should talk to an attorney or other knowledgeable advisor. This is a big financial decision with long-term consequences, so it's worth spending a few hundred bucks to get it right.*

As a general matter, though, even in states where they can, many lenders don't bother to pursue deficiency judgments unless they have some reason to think that the homeowner has money to pay one. It can be costly to pursue a deficiency judgment and your lender is primarily concerned about maximizing its profit. So, it's unlikely to pursue a deficiency judgment if the money that it could possibly recover from you is less than what it would cost to get the judgment in the first place. Indeed, if you're worried about a deficiency judgment because you don't have the money to pay one, you may be worrying for no reason. If your lender knows that you don't have the money, it's unlikely to bother.

Occasionally, of course, lenders do pursue homeowners for deficiency judgments. When they do, they sometimes like to make a big deal of it, which is why you sometimes see news stories about lenders pursuing homeowners. The idea is that other homeowners will see those stories and be scared in disproportion to the actual risk. In other words, lenders play upon the salience of these stories and the human tendency to overestimate risk of isolated incidents that we read about in the newspapers or hear on TV. For example, people are apt to think plane accidents are more likely than they actually are after hearing about one on the news, even when the risk of plane accidents hasn't increased at all.

Just because you read about some lender pursuing some poor homeowner in New Jersey, doesn't mean that the risk of your being pursued has increased at all. YouWalkAway.com reports that only .1% of the over 4,000 people that it has helped default have been pursued for a deficiency judgment. Nevertheless, there is some risk, and one cannot say whether the YouWalkAway.com numbers are representative of the risk for you. Your risk of a deficiency judgment will vary according to your state, your loan type, and your lender.

Some lenders may also try to identify whether you're a "strategic defaulter" by looking at your credit report. By "strategic defaulter," lenders mean someone who defaults without hardship, which, strictly speaking, is an inaccurate definition of strategic default. Default is strategic if you deliberately choose it, hardship or not. But lenders seem to reserve special disdain for those homeowners who they think can "afford" their mortgages. If the only loan that you've defaulted on or had any late payments on is your mortgage, then your lender *may* suspect that you're a "strategic defaulter." As such, you may want to let your lender know if you're in bad financial shape and facing a genuine hardship. If your bank knows that you're deeply in debt and have no savings, it's probably less likely to pursue a deficiency judgment, as it wouldn't be financially worthwhile to do so.

If you don't want to share your financial information with your lender, you may want to think about how you allocate your limited financial resources each month. You may decide to pay your mortgage some months and not others. Pay some bills some months and other bills other months. If you do this, the bank's screening system may tell it that you're a "cash-flow manager," not a strategic defaulter. Moreover, if you default on all or most of your bills, the bank's screening system will likely tell it that you're experiencing significant financial hardship and there's little chance that you'll be singled out. This should give you some comfort if you're like most homeowners considering default and are, in fact, facing financial hardship.

You should, of course, do what makes you feel the most comfortable in choosing how or when to pay your bills. But you might like to know that "cash-flow management" is a skill that they teach at business school. Just like with a lot of other things, we seem to have two sets of rules in this country: one for individuals and another for corporations. As individuals, we're told that we should always pay our debts on time. But corporations routinely, as a matter of "cash-flow management," intentionally wait to pay their bills until they are 90 days or more late and their creditors call to demand payment. It's just business to corporations. Keeping cash on hand as long as possible allows them to use it to make more money.

The disadvantage of this approach for you is that, unlike corporations which are financially rewarded for cash-flow management, it will do much more damage to your credit score than stopping mortgage payments alone. Additionally, though it may reduce your chances of being singled out rightly or wrongly as someone defaulting without financial hardship, cash-flow management may not be necessary to prevent your bank from knowing your personal situation. If you just stop paying your mortgage and nothing else, you could be doing so because you lost your job. Or you could be doing it because you had to move, or got a divorce. You may, in fact, be suffering substantial hardship and have decided that, all things considered, it's better to default on your mortgage than your other debts. Indeed, most people who default on their mortgage are in exactly that situation.

That said, if your lender believes that you're defaulting with no hardship at all, it's more likely to pursue you for a deficiency judgment, though perhaps not much more likely. The risk of being pursued for a deficiency judgment is also higher for a home equity line of credit (HELOC) if it was not used to purchase your home. Non-purchase money HELOCs are full-recourse loans even in states that are non-recourse for purchase money mortgages. Cash-out refinances are also typically full-recourse loans. This makes sense. If someone has used the equity in their home to send their children to college, to finance a business, or to buy other things, the case for making the loan "non-recourse" is less compelling than it is for a purchase money mortgage, which is used only for the purchase of the house.

A homeowner with a non-purchase money HELOC or cash-out refinance is underwater not just because the housing market collapsed, but because they used their equity for other things. There's nothing wrong with having done so. But if they hadn't, they might not be underwater. This difference is why even non-recourse states only prohibit deficiency judgments for purchase money mortgages, and sometimes straight refinances that don't take cash out. If a loan wasn't used for one's house, then a decrease in the value of one's house arguably isn't relevant to one's obligation to repay the loan.

Defaulting on a HELOC is, in many ways, similar to defaulting on a credit card— and a credit card company can pursue you if you default.

The fact that a lender can pursue you for a deficiency judgment doesn't mean that it actually will; just that it may. In addition, they may sell the right to pursue you to someone else, usually for pennies on the dollar. That said, you might be able to convince your HELOC lender to release any claim it may have for a deficiency as part of a short sale. If not, and if you're pursued for a deficiency judgment, you may be able to settle for much less than the actual deficiency. Think of all the commercials that you hear about settling credit card debt for less than owed. It's possible to settle debt for less because it's usually cheaper for credit card companies than trying to pursue a debtor in court. It's the same with your HELOC.

Additionally, you may be able to use the threat of bankruptcy or actual bankruptcy to help you in this negotiation. Indeed, you should keep in the back of your mind that bankruptcy might provide important protection for you in the event that your lender does pursue you for a deficiency judgment. A deficiency judgment is unsecured debt, which means that it can be discharged or substantially reduced in bankruptcy. Moreover, bankruptcy will allow you to reduce or eliminate other debt as well, including credit card debt, auto loans, and personal debt. Indeed, bankruptcy can be a great way to get back on your feet again if you find yourself buried in debt. Even if bankruptcy sounds unappealing to you, it can be part of your back-up plan. You don't have to file it, but it may be there if you need it—even if you probably won't.

Your lender is using the legal system to its advantage and you can, too, as did this former underwater homeowner who shared her story with me:

> As for the effect on me after deciding to walk, I knew the foreclosure would hurt my credit rating for a while. However, I continued to remain current on other debt obligations, including personal lines of credit and a credit card. After HSBC started pursuing me for the $40,000 I owed it on the second deed of trust, I then decided a year later to file for Chapter 7 bankruptcy... Bottom line: my credit score remains in the 600s and I obtained a personal loan a few months ago through my credit union. My debts total under $8,000, credit cards included, so I am not doing wild spending nor living above my means. Currently, I rent, and I am happy to continue to do so for the foreseeable future. – M.S.

Even if you have significant assets or income such that bankruptcy wouldn't be a viable option, there are steps you may be able to take that can help protect you and your assets from a deficiency judgment. Corporations use various legal structures to shield their assets and protect themselves from liability as a regular part of doing business. You have a right to protect yourself as well. You should consult with an attorney to discuss your options.

In short, although there may be some risk of a deficiency judgment if you default on your mortgage, it may be a risk worth taking. Think of it this way. Imagine that you're underwater by $200,000 and your total monthly cost of owning is twice what you pay to rent a comparable home. In such a case, you may save well over $200,000 by voluntarily giving up your home to foreclosure. Now let's say that after consulting with an attorney about your loan type, your state's laws, and your personal situation, you figure that the risk of a deficiency judgment is about 2%. That means that your expected loss is $200,000 X .02, or $4,000, but your expected gain from foreclosure is over $200,000. If you were a business, it's clear which one you'd choose.

But you're not a business. Thus, even a small chance of a deficiency judgment may be too much for you. How much risk is too much depends on your personal tolerance for risk. But, in making your decision, you should rely upon facts and accurate information rather than exaggerated stories from those who have an interest in making you feel much more afraid than you may need to be.

Concern for Credit Score

The other major cost associated with default is damaging your credit score. If you really care about your credit score, what I am about to tell you may be hard to believe. But your credit score is probably worth much less than you think. The credit industry has devoted a lot of money to convincing us to see our credit scores as a statement of our human worth. We've been told that our credit score reflects our moral character, our sense of personal responsibility, and our trustworthiness. We've been so conditioned that even having our credit card incorrectly turned down at a store can feel deeply humiliating.

The first thing that you have to do if you're going to default is to stop buying into this nonsense. As long as you're emotionally attached to your credit score, or see it as a reflection of you as a person, your lender will be able to threaten your credit score to constrain your behavior and to gain the upper hand in negotiations over your mortgage.

As an illustration, if you call your lender to work out a loan modification and you have a good credit score and solid mortgage payment history, you may be told, or it may be implied, that your lender will not discuss a loan modification until you're 30 days or more delinquent on your mortgage payment. Your lender may tell you that loan modifications are for people who can't make their payments and not for people who can. If you haven't defaulted, your lender will conclude that you can pay your mortgage. The lender may also bet that you value your credit score too much to miss a payment and that you will just give up the idea of a loan modification.

However, if you miss a payment and call back to discuss a loan modification in 30 days, your lender may tell you it can't talk to you until you're 90 days delinquent. In the meantime, your lender may send you strongly-worded notices warning that you face "imminent foreclosure." You may also start getting phone calls in which the lender will lecture you about your moral obligation to pay your mortgage and will threaten you with foreclosure and a deficiency judgment if you don't bring your mortgage payments current.

Your lender may make this threat even if you live in a non-recourse state and it can't pursue you for a deficiency judgment. It may also make the threat if you live in recourse state, but it in fact has no intention whatsoever of pursuing such a judgment. Indeed, the person calling you likely has no decision-making authority at all and is just following a script. In following this script, the caller may also tell you about the huge tax bill you will face, even if you don't face one at all. And he or she will almost certainly tell you that a foreclosure will "destroy" your credit.

Your lender will again be making a bet that you can be shamed or frightened into paying your mortgage. If you proceed undeterred and call back when you're 90 days delinquent, there's a good possibility that you'll be told that your credit score is now so low that you don't qualify for a loan modification. Your lender will be hoping that you'll be discouraged and will start paying your mortgage again to save your house from foreclosure. If you somehow make clear to the lender that you have chosen foreclosure, the lender *may* finally be willing to negotiate a loan modification, a short-sale or a deed-in-lieu of foreclosure.

Most lenders will, in other words, take full advantage of your moral reservations about defaulting on your mortgage and will use the threat of damaging your credit score to bring you into compliance. Additionally, many lenders will only bargain with you when the threat of damaging your credit has plainly lost its force and it becomes clear to the lender that foreclosure is imminent absent some accommodation. On a fundamental level, your lender counts on the fact that you and it are playing by different rules. Your lender counts on your being motivated by moral norms and emotions—such as shame, guilt, and fear—while it's motivated only by profits. This difference in rules gives your lender an unfair advantage in the negotiation. Your hands are tied behind your back, and your lender is punching you in the face.

Unless you want to be beaten down by your lender, you have to untie your hands and let go of your attachment to your credit score. Even though it may feel like it, a credit score isn't a scarlet letter. It says nothing about your moral character. Many hardworking, honest, responsible Americans have low credit scores. Things happen. People lose their jobs, especially in this economy. People get sick. Family members have emergencies and need our help. There are an endless number of events in life that can make it impossible to pay the bills and can lead to a low credit score. None of these things make you a bad person.

Having a low credit score because life's circumstances dealt you a heavy blow says absolutely nothing about your moral character or your worth as a human being. One of the worst financial blows that you can suffer is for your primary asset – your home – to lose half its value. If you need to default on your mortgage to save yourself from financial disaster, that doesn't make you a bad person. You didn't cause the housing market to collapse. If you need to default to protect your family, doing so doesn't make you irresponsible. To the contrary, it may be the most responsible thing that you can do for your family.

You should know, in fact, that corporations that default on their mortgages are considered good investments on Wall Street. The Wall Street Journal recently reported, for example, that real estate development companies that default on their underwater properties are given *higher* investment ratings than those who don't. On Wall Street, companies that default on their mortgages are considered wisely-managed. As a result of their defaulting, their investment rating goes up! Yet, you're told that you're irresponsible if you default, and your credit score goes down.

In addition to conditioning us to feel that our credit score reflects our moral character, the credit industry devotes a great deal of resources to scare us into thinking that a low credit score threatens our very survival. That's the whole point of companies like FreeCreditScore.com, which run ads on TV telling us that if our credit score is bad, we'll end up living in our in-laws' basement. The credit industry also benefits from personal finance media pundits who tell their readers that mortgage default delivers a "knockout blow to the homeowner's credit" and ripples "through every corner of borrowers' financial lives."

If you believed these pundits, a bad credit score as a result of default and foreclosure pretty much spells disaster for you. In reality, just how much an initial impact a foreclosure has on one's credit is unclear because the credit rating companies will not share this information. Uncertainty breeds fear, so the credit rating companies like to keep the secret to your credit score in a mysterious black box, and to keep you anxious that any wrong step will damage it irreparably. But generally you can expect a 100- to 150-point hit to your credit score as a result of a foreclosure, and an additional hit for falling 90 days delinquent. Additionally, you must wait seven years for the foreclosure to disappear completely from your credit report.

But assuming you have otherwise good credit, and continue to meet you other credit obligations, it's possible to have a good—or even great—credit rating again within two years after a foreclosure. Indeed, many people have a great credit score within months of foreclosure. Additionally, in as little as three years, you can qualify for a federally-insured FHA loan to purchase another home – as long as you can show "extenuating circumstances," such as medical bills, loss of income, unemployment, birth of a child, or other change that contributed to the foreclosure. For most people, identifying an extenuating circumstance shouldn't be very hard to do. You're probably facing at least one. You can also reasonably bet that if you have a great credit score again in a few years, there will be plenty of other lenders out there willing to give you a loan.

Moreover, if you already have a low credit score because you have been struggling to pay the bills, hanging on to your house to protect your credit score makes little sense at all. In fact, if you have a low credit score and you use the extra money from defaulting to pay down your other debts, defaulting on your mortgage may actually make your credit score go up. One of the biggest determinants of your credit score is your debt utilization ratio, meaning how much of your available credit you're using. So if you pay down your debt, your credit score may very well go up. The key is to be disciplined and use the opportunity of not paying your mortgage to right your financial ship by paying down your other debt.

That said, the hit to your credit score from default and foreclosure is real. And it can be significant. Credit card companies also sometimes reduce people's available credit after they default. This can cause your credit score to decline even because your debt utilization ratio may rise if you have less credit available. However, because of recent credit card reforms, credit card companies cannot jack up your interest rates on existing debt just because you defaulted on your mortgage. They used to be able to do so, but not anymore. Nevertheless, if you're going to default, you should be prepared for a few years of limited access to credit.

The actual financial cost of having a low credit score for a few years is hard to quantify, but it's not likely to be significant for most individuals, especially not when compared to the savings from shedding a seriously underwater property. Indeed, even MSN columnist Liz Pullam Weston, who has made a nice living telling people how important their credit scores are, estimates that a *lifetime* of bad credit costs only $201,000. That's a little under $3000 per year if you live to be 70. But remember, you're only looking at 2 to 3 years, at most, until your credit score recovers. You may recover within months. Moreover, Weston's scenario is based upon someone who buys a *lifetime* of cars on bad credit, takes student loans on bad credit, and carries a large balance on high interest credit cards for their *whole life* on bad credit. In other words, she, like many others, exaggerates the cost of a low credit score. Unless you are in some unique circumstance, then you can expect that a few years of a low credit score won't cost more than a couple thousand dollars, and maybe much less. Moreover, you can take steps to minimize even this marginal cost. For example, as discussed above, you can purchase a vehicle or other necessities *before* you default and just avoid using credit for a few years.

Also, you shouldn't overlook family resources that can help you through the time of limited access to credit. For example, you may have family members who are able and willing to be there in a pinch if you need them. This in itself can give someone peace of mind. Additionally, as long as you have money in your bank account, you can use a debit card for most things for which you might have used a credit card. Finally, as long as you keep making your payments on your credit cards, your credit card companies are unlikely to cancel your cards.

That said, if you're in a position where you need access to significant credit in the next few years, then default may not be for you. For example, if you have a child going off to college soon and will need to take out loans to send them to college, default could be costly. You, of course, shouldn't assume that defaulting will keep you from paying for your child's college, as there may be ways around the issue. For example, if you save thousands a year by defaulting, that may be enough either alone or combined with other resources to pay the tuition. You should also contact the financial aid office of the school that your child wishes to attend and ask them how they help students attend school when their parents are unable to take out loans. They likely deal with this situation frequently and may offer some guidance and reassurance. Make your decision based upon facts, not fear.

As another word of caution, if you're in one of the *few* professions where your credit report matters for security clearance, then default may not be for you. Many people who have this concern, however, learn after they look into it that default and foreclosure will only affect their security clearance if they hide it. Disclosure is often enough to avoid any problems.

Default also may not be the choice for you if you're looking for a job in some field where employers are likely to check credit reports. But, again, don't let fear of prospective employers checking your credit report drive your decision-making. It's possible that a negative credit report could be an issue for a few employers, but the reality is that most prospective employers don't check credit reports. If they do, they have to tell you beforehand. You can explain that you had to let go of your home because of financial hardship—which, if you're looking for a job, probably includes being unemployed. By being forthright about your situation, you demonstrate your honesty, and most employers are unlikely to hold a negative credit report against you.

At the very least, before assuming the worst, do some research to see if employers in your particular occupation check credit reports. Call employers in your occupation and ask. If they check credit reports, ask them (without giving your name) whether losing your home to foreclosure would affect your chances of employment. After you've done this research, you can then make an informed decision. If you're unemployed and your credit score is already low, remember that defaulting and paying off your other debt may actually increase your credit score. If you already have a job, and your job is secure, your credit score will probably recover before you ever have to look for employment again, anyway.

The bottom line is that your credit score isn't as important as the credit industry would like you to believe, and it doesn't define you as a person. It's a credit industry invention used in part to control your behavior. Don't be held hostage by fear or shame. If you need a good credit score in the next few years for some concrete reason, then maybe you shouldn't default. But if you can live without easy access to credit for a few years, or your credit score is already low, protecting your credit score isn't a very good reason to keep paying your underwater mortgage — especially if it threatens your family's financial future.

Worry about Tax Consequences

Another common scare tactic used to control homeowners is to tell them that will face a "huge" tax bill if they give up their house to foreclosure. Like a lot of other scary stories about foreclosure, this one is mostly untrue as well. As mentioned above, the Mortgage Debt Forgiveness Relief Act of 2007 provides that you do not have to pay taxes on forgiven debt that was incurred to purchase or improve your primary residence.

As a general matter, it's true that if you borrow money from a commercial lender and the lender agrees to forgive the debt, you're required to pay taxes on the amount forgiven because that amount is treated as income to you. It's as if the lender gave you the money to pay off the loan. As such, when a lender forgives or "writes-off" the debt they are required to report the "discharged debt" to the federal government as income to you, which they do on a 1099 form. As the IRS explains in this example: "You borrow $10,000 and default on the loan after paying back $2,000. If the lender is unable to collect the remaining debt from you, there is a cancellation of debt of $8,000, which generally is taxable income to you." In other words, before the enactment of the Mortgage Debt Forgiveness Relief Act, you would have been required to pay taxes on any portion of your mortgage that your lender did not recover from the foreclosure sale or from you personally.

The Mortgage Debt Forgiveness Relief Act, however, generally allows you to exclude from income "discharged debt" on your principal residence as long as the debt was "used to buy, build or substantially improve your principal residence, or to refinance debt incurred for those purposes." Moreover, you can exclude up to $2 million of discharged primary residence debt if you're married and $1 million if you're single. This includes debt forgiven as a result of a loan modification, short-sale, or a foreclosure. You can find out more about the Mortgage Debt Forgiveness Relief Act on the IRS website. The Mortgage Debt Forgiveness Relief Act expires at the end of 2011, so you should keep that in mind in making your decision.

You should also be aware that the Mortgage Debt Forgiveness Relief Act doesn't apply to loans used for things other than purchasing, building, or improving your primary residence. For example, if you took out a home equity line of credit (HELOC) to pay for your child's college, you will have to pay taxes on that loan if it's discharged by your lender. Rather than be concerned about this, however, you should realize that it's a great thing if your lender discharges the debt. Paying taxes on the resulting "income" from the discharged debt is *a lot* cheaper than paying the entire debt.

The Mortgage Debt Forgiveness Relief Act aside, discharged debt on non-recourse loans has long been nontaxable as income. As the IRS explains, "forgiveness of a non-recourse loan resulting from a foreclosure does not result in cancellation of debt income." In other words, if you live in an anti-deficiency judgment state and your lender's only recourse is to take your house, then it isn't forgiving any debt. To the contrary, the loan is fully satisfied when the lender takes the house. Thus, there's no debt to forgive.

Additionally, debts discharged through bankruptcy aren't taxable, which is another reason that you may want to consider bankruptcy to force a modification of mortgages on your rental properties or to eliminate second and third mortgages on your primary residence for a fraction of what you owe. This strategy will be discussed in more detail later in "Weighing your Options."

You should, of course, consult with a professional to determine the exact tax consequences of defaulting on your mortgage. But by no means should you just believe those who claim that you will face a huge tax bill if you default. By now, you can probably see the pattern: those who want to keep you from considering default throw out a list of terrible consequences, most of which aren't true or are half-truths. If the list is long enough, they figure you'll just run in the other direction and clean out your retirement account, or whatever else is necessary, to pay your mortgage. To fight back against this tactic, you must commit to basing your decision on facts and not fear. Yes, default has consequences, but the consequences are rarely disastrous and frequently quite manageable.

Chapter 3: Financial Dimensions

If you already know that you're significantly underwater and that it would make financial sense to default, you can skip ahead to the next chapter, "Weighing Your Options." But I would recommend coming back to read this chapter, because sometimes it may make sense to keep paying your mortgage even if you're underwater.

Are You Underwater, and by How Much?

Despite everything discussed previously, the first thing that you need to do before making any decision is to figure out whether you're actually underwater. In other words, do you really owe more on your house than it's worth? And, if so, how much? Figuring out if you're underwater isn't always easy. It's also an unpleasant task. Things are ugly out there and it's a lot more enjoyable to think about other things. But, if you haven't already, you owe it to yourself and your family to take your head out of the sand and take a good, hard look at what your house is really worth.

For most of us, it's very hard to accept that our home is worth less than we paid, much less hundreds of thousands of dollars less. Because we don't want to deal with the distress of being underwater, we sometimes fool ourselves into thinking that our homes are worth more than they actually are. For example, one study found that homeowners tend to overestimate their homes' values by about 10%. Homeowners are especially likely to overestimate the value of their homes if they bought their houses during a boom, with such homeowners overestimating their homes' values by more than 20%.

We overestimate our homes' values in part because we tend to see what we want to see. For example, we may notice list prices of over-priced homes in our neighborhood, instead of actual sales prices. We also tend to think our own homes are nicer than similar houses in the neighborhood, even when objectively speaking they are not. We also tend to discount media reports of steep price declines as somehow inapplicable to our particular neighborhood. You may love your house and your neighborhood. But on the housing market, your house is just a commodity, worth only what similar commodities are worth.

Additionally, if your primary exposure to the housing market came when you bought during the bubble, the high prices during the bubble will loom large in your mind. You understand that prices have come down, but the natural human tendency is to "anchor" to the price that you paid for your house and then "under-discount" from that price. In other words, you're likely to underestimate how much prices have fallen and to overestimate your own home's value.

For this reason, it's important to use an objective measure in determining the value of your house. You shouldn't decide what your house is worth based upon your own sense of its value. You should leave it to others who are not emotionally involved. One way to do this is to look on websites such as www.zillow.com or the *Home Price Calculator* on www.fhfa.gov where you can put in the address of your home and get an estimate of its current value.

If these numbers come back lower than you think they should, resist the natural urge to discount them because you don't like the message. The common tendency is for people to argue in their head with information that they don't like until they convince themselves that the information isn't true. For example, I've heard people discount Zillow.com on the grounds that Zillow's estimates are based upon averages in your neighborhood and don't take into account the special characteristics of your home. But the Zillow estimate is based in part on what your home sold for before. So it does take into account some of your home's unique characteristics.

Nevertheless, you shouldn't rely upon one source of information, which is why you should also look at the home price calculator on www.fhfa.gov. You should seek out other estimates as well. Ideally, you should get an opinion from an independent appraiser. Indeed, with such a big decision ahead of you, getting an objective appraisal could be more than worth what you'd pay for it.

If you can't afford a professional estimate, you can estimate what your house is worth yourself based upon its rental value. This is because a basic principle of economics is that the value of a home, even an owner-occupied one, is "the current value of the rent payments that could be earned from renting the property at market prices." People lost sight of this in the housing bubble, which is a big part of why things got out of hand.

But the calculation isn't as simple as comparing total mortgage payments to rent payments. Home ownership, unlike renting, carries certain benefits including tax breaks and the potential for appreciation. Additionally, the portion of the mortgage payment that goes to principal rather than interest will, in a non-depreciating market, eventually come back to you at the time of sale. You'll never get your rent back. On the flip side, homeownership carries significant risks and costs that renting does not — including maintenance, homeowners insurance, the risk of depreciation, and substantial transaction costs upon selling.

If your head is hurting from trying to figure out how to weigh all these factors, don't despair. There's an easy formula for figuring out how much your house is worth based upon its rental value. It's called the price-to-rent ratio. The national average price-to-rent ratio over the last 15 years has been roughly 16:1. In other words, as a national average, if a house would rent for $1000 a month, or $12,000 a year, the price to purchase that home would be $12,000 x 16, or $192,000. The price-to-rent ratio varies by city, however, so ideally you should find the ratio for your particular city. Below is a chart listing the 15-year average of price-to-rent ratios in 54 cities. If your city isn't on the list, choose a similar nearby city or use the national ratio.

Price-to-Rent Ratios

City	15 year average	City	15 year average
NATIONAL AVERAGE	**16.9**	Miami	16.0
Atlanta	14.8	Milwaukee	18.1
Austin	16.3	Minneapolis	15.5
Baltimore	12.6	Nashville	20.5
Boston	18.0	New Orleans	14.8
Charlotte	18.2	New York	11.7
Chicago	18.3	Norfolk	17.9
Cincinnati	15.1	Oklahoma City	12.7
Cleveland	14.3	Orange County, Calif.	24.3
Columbus	16.9	Orlando	14.9
Dallas	16.1	Palm Beach County, Fla.	17.6
Denver	19.1	Philadelphia	12.5
Detroit	10.9	Phoenix	14.0
East Bay, Calif./Oakland	31.6	Pittsburgh	10.6

Fort Lauderdale	15.7	Portland, Ore.	20.8
Greater Kansas City	14.8	Raleigh	19.4
Greater Washington, D.C.	15.9	Richmond	16.8
Hartford	14.9	Sacramento	19.4
Honolulu	25.5	Salt Lake City	16.3
Houston	14.3	San Antonio	13.5
Indianapolis	14.9	San Diego	22.4
Inland Empire, Calif.	18.8	San Francisco	27.4
Jacksonville	14.3	San Jose	27.2
Las Vegas	18.9	Seattle	23.3
Long Island, N.Y.	15.7	St. Louis	14.0
Los Angeles	16.0	Stamford, Conn.	22.0
Memphis	18.1	Tampa	14.5

Once you know your city's price-to-rent ratio or a close approximation, you can figure out the approximate value of your home by multiplying the monthly rent times 12 and multiplying that times the price-to-rent ratio in your city. The result is a rough approximation of what your house is fundamentally worth. If you don't know your house's rental value, you can see what similar houses rent for by looking online or in the newspaper. Or, call rental management companies and ask for estimates.

As a word of caution, home prices in your city may currently be higher or lower than the historic price-to-rent ratio. Some economists argue that prices are likely to rise or fall until they're in line with the historic ratio. Under this reasoning, home prices may continue to decline in cities where current home prices exceed the historic rent-to-price ratio, as homes are still overpriced. On the other hand, homes in cities where home prices are lower than the historic price-to-rent ratio may begin to increase in value, as they are underpriced.

Following this line of thinking, it wouldn't make financial sense to default on your mortgage if the amount that you owe is less than the house is worth according to the historic price-to-rent ratio. Even if home prices are lower in your market right now than this ratio, they're likely to come back. On the other hand, if you owe significantly more than your house is worth according to the historic price-to-rent ratio, it may be many years before your house is worth what you owe.

You shouldn't rely upon the price-to-rent ratio alone to determine your home's value. You should also look at www.zillow.com or www.fhfa.gov, or get an independent opinion from a qualified appraiser or an unbiased real estate agent. If the various estimates from these sources more or less line up, you can be pretty confident that you know what your house is worth. If the numbers are all over the place, disregard the extremes (both high and low). Or go with the value based on the current or historic price-to-rent ratio, depending on which is the most relevant to you. Once you have a reasonable estimate of your home's value, compare it to the balance(s) on your most recent mortgage statement(s) including home equity lines. If the total balance is more than your house is worth, then you're underwater.

Are You Paying too Much for a Place to Live?

Just because you're underwater doesn't mean that you should necessarily panic or default on your mortgage. It may not feel good to be underwater, but sometimes it makes financial sense to stay and keep paying your mortgage, anyway. First of all, there are costs to default that you should take into account. These include moving costs, the cost of a low credit score (however temporary), the risk of a deficiency judgment and the psychological costs of losing your home and moving away from your neighborhood.

These are real costs and have led some commentators to suggest that it doesn't make sense to start thinking of defaulting until you're about 10% underwater. That's probably about right for most homeowners. On the other hand, people tend to undervalue long term gains and overvalue short term losses. For example, you may so dread the thought of moving that it drowns out thoughts of the thousands of dollars that you may save from giving up your home, and all the benefits that extra money may bring to you in the future. Because we tend to compartmentalize our thinking, it's easy to lose sight of the fact that the costs of moving may be minimal when compared to the long-term benefits of saving tens of thousands of dollars.

But, you've got to live somewhere. And if you default on your mortgage, you'll probably have to rent. *If your net cost of owning is less than what you'd pay for rent, then you should probably just stay where you are, and ride it out.*

In order to figure out if your net monthly cost of owning is less than what you'd pay for rent, you're going to have to do some math. You're also going to have to gather some information and do some research. There's just no way around this if you want to make an informed decision. It's like figuring out your taxes; it's not pleasant, but you'd be foolish not to do it. Also, like taxes, if you don't want to do it by yourself, you can hire a professional to help you.

If you want to save some money and figure it out yourself, the next few sections will walk you through it. We'll take it step-by-step. In order to calculate your net monthly cost of owning, you first need to calculate your gross monthly cost. Your gross monthly cost isn't just your mortgage principal and interest payment; it also includes maintenance expenses, homeowners insurance, mortgage insurance, homeowners' association dues, taxes and other miscellaneous expenses. Your monthly mortgage payment probably includes homeowners insurance, mortgage insurance, and taxes. But it doesn't include maintenance expenses, homeowners' association dues, and other expenses such as a pool or yard service. So you'll need to add these additional expenses to your monthly payment to figure out your total average monthly costs:

_____	Mortgage payment (PMI, homeowners insurance and property taxes)
+_____	Average Monthly Maintenance
+_____	Homeowners Association Dues
+_____	Other (yard service, pool service, etc…)
=_____	Gross Monthly Cost of Owning

Once you calculate your gross monthly cost, you'll need to subtract the home interest tax deduction from this total to figure out your net monthly cost of owning. Figuring out the tax deduction is tricky, as everyone is entitled to a standard tax deduction, which for married couples filing a joint return is $11,400 and for individuals is $5,700 in 2010. But to get the mortgage interest deduction, you have to itemize your deductions, and you lose the standard deduction. Thus, you only benefit from the mortgage interest deduction to the extent that your mortgage interest payments, plus other itemized deductions, exceed the standard deduction. This may come as a surprise to you, because homebuyers are frequently told when they purchase their homes that they can deduct mortgage interest on their taxes, which is technically true. But it's rarely explained that you must give up the standard deduction in order to do so, nor is the impact of giving up the standard deduction explained.

To figure out how much of an actual tax break you're getting as a result of your mortgage interest, use the worksheet below. To get the information that you need for this worksheet, take a look at your itemized deductions (including mortgage interest) on your last tax return and subtract the standard deduction. The amount remaining after you subtract the standard deduction is how much of your mortgage interest results in an actual deduction. If your non-mortgage related itemized deductions exceed the standard deduction, all the mortgage interest results in an actual deduction. In either event, take the actual deduction and multiply it by your marginal tax rate. The result is your actual annual yearly tax break from owning. Divide this number by twelve to get your monthly tax break. Here is a worksheet:

Mortgage Interest Monthly Tax Break Worksheet

Do your *non-mortgage related* itemized deductions exceed $11,400 if you're married or $5,700 if you're single?

If no, calculate your monthly mortgage interest tax break here:

```
_____ Total Itemized Deductions
           (including mortgage interest)
- _____ Standard Deduction
  _____ (Subtotal)
x _____ Marginal tax rate (e.g., .28)
  _____ Annual Mortgage Tax Savings
÷  12   _ Number of months in tax year
= _____ Monthly tax break
```

If yes, calculate your monthly mortgage interest tax break here:

```
_____ Yearly Mortgage Interest
x _____ Marginal tax rate (e.g., .28)
_____ Annual Mortgage Tax Savings
÷  12   _ Number of months in tax year
= _____ Monthly tax break
```

Now, to figure out the net monthly cost of owning, deduct the monthly tax break from the gross monthly cost from above:

       _____ Gross Monthly Cost of Owning
\-   _____ Monthly tax break
=   _____ Net Monthly Cost of Owning

If your net monthly cost of owning is less, the same, or only slightly more than it would cost to rent your house, you're paying the fair market price for a place to live. You're not wasting your money because you'd have to spend that money on rent anyway. What's more, none of your rent ever comes back and the portion of your mortgage payment that goes to principal will, as long as your home doesn't depreciate faster than you can pay down your mortgage. That's why it can be financially rational to pay a little more in total monthly costs to own than to rent, even if you're underwater. If rent would cost the same as owning on a monthly basis, there's no pressing financial reason to default on your mortgage. However, if your net monthly cost of owning *significantly* exceeds what you would pay to rent a comparable place, then you may want to do some additional calculations to figure out whether continuing to pay your mortgage makes financial sense for you. We'll talk about those calculations after the next section.

Do You Need to Move?

The above calculation is a bit different if you need to move. First, if you need to move for a new job and are considering not taking the job because of your underwater house, you need to add the difference between what you're making now, if anything, and what you would make at your new job. Then add that difference to the net monthly cost of owning, because if you're turning down a job because of your underwater home, you may not only be paying too much for a place to live, but you're losing the salary that you could be making as well.

Before you default, however, you should think about renting out your house. If you can rent your house out for more than the net monthly cost of owning, then it *may* make sense to become a landlord instead of defaulting, even if you're underwater. But in figuring whether to become a landlord, you should calculate that you will have to pay about 10% of the rent to a management company, unless you want to manage the rental from afar. In addition, you need to figure in one or two months a year when the house may be vacant. You also need to think about the hassles of finding tenants.

On the bright side, you can deduct depreciation of 4% each year on your taxes if the house is a rental (structure only, not land). You may also deduct mortgage interest and repairs as expenses. You need to make sure that you factor this deduction into the equation when deciding whether you can cover your total monthly expenses with the rent. Sometimes the 4% deduction for depreciation can make renting your house financially viable even though it does not initially appear to be the case. However, you can currently only deduct up to $25,000 a year on a rental. The deduction is phased out as your taxable income exceeds $100,000 until disappearing if your taxable income is $150,000 or more. If you're thinking of renting out your home, you'd be wise to talk to an accountant and do some careful planning.

The bottom line is that your house would need to rent for significantly more than the total monthly cost of owning before you could rent your house out without losing money. Additionally, if you're thinking of giving up a job opportunity to stay in your underwater home, you should add any salary increase that you're foregoing to the monthly cost of owning.

The Costs of Doing Nothing

If you're underwater and paying significantly more on a monthly basis than you would to rent, then it may very well make financial sense to give up your house. How much sense it would make, if any, is an individualized, complex and state-specific calculation. This section will help you identify the factors that you should consider and how you might think about weighing them.

The first step is figuring out how much you would save by shedding your mortgage. One way to go about this is to use an online calculator designed for this purpose such as the YouWalkAway.com calculator. The YouWalkAway.com calculator can quickly provide you with a rough estimate of what you may save by renting instead of continuing to pay your mortgage, with the most useful numbers being the *Walk Away Cash Savings* and the *Net Monthly Savings*. It's certainly worth checking out the YouWalkAway.com calculator, and running several different scenarios.

This section will explain a more precise, but still rough, method for estimating what you could save by renting instead of continuing to pay your mortgage. This method will require some more mathematical calculations, and will require you to make an educated guess as to what future appreciation is likely to be for your house (though you'll need to estimate future appreciation with the YouWalkAway.com calculator as well). Then, using this estimate, along with the current value of your house, your current principal balance, and your net monthly savings from renting, you can estimate both how long until you will be above water and how much it will cost you to wait it out until then. From earlier calculations, you should already have the current value of your home, your current principal balance, and your net monthly savings from renting (which is the amount by which the net monthly costs of owning exceeds the monthly rental value of your home).

Next, you need to make an educated guess as to future appreciation for your house. You should probably be somewhat conservative in doing so, as homeowners tend toward optimistic overconfidence believing that home prices will bounce back in a few years and that their homes will soon be worth more than they paid. Indeed, optimistic overconfidence may have led many homeowners to take out interest-only adjustable-rate mortgages ("ARMs") in the misplaced belief that they would have better salaries in a few years or would refinance as their homes' values grew. The housing collapse has taught us all the dangers of optimistic overconfidence.

Most economists believe that the housing market will be slow to recover and that appreciation will be below the historical average, which is 3- 4% a year, for quite a while in many markets – particularly if inflation stays low. Economists have certainly been wrong before, and they could be wrong again. You might also strike it rich in Las Vegas. But you may not want to bet your family's financial future on it. So you may want to be conservative and not use a number larger than 3 or 4% for expected appreciation. Moreover, you should be careful even in using 3 or

4% if prices aren't yet going up in your area or are still declining. In such case, you might select 2%. To get a better sense of your particular housing market, do some online research.

With your estimate of appreciation in hand, you can estimate how many years it will be until you're no longer underwater on your mortgage - or your *"above water mark."* To do this, run an amortization chart on your mortgage (http://www.easycalculation.com/mortgage/amortization.php). The amortization chart will tell you the rate at which you will pay off your mortgage and how much you will owe year-by-year. Then, you can estimate how much your house will be worth year-by-year if it appreciates at the rate that you predict. There's no calculator online specifically designed for estimating year by year home appreciation, but you can run a compound interest chart (http://www.math.com/students/calculators/source/compound.htm), using the current value of the house as the initial balance, your estimated appreciation as the percent yield, 30 as the number of years, and zero as the monthly contribution. The result is how much your house will be worth if it appreciates at the rate you entered, and the compound interest chart will tell you the value of your home year-by-year. Finally, compare the two charts to see when the value of your house (represented by the compound interest chart) will exceed the amount you owe on your mortgage (as indicated on the amortization chart). That would be the *above water mark.*

To get a rough estimate of how much you would save by renting instead of owning during this time, multiply your net monthly savings from renting by 12 to get the yearly savings, and then multiply that by the number of years until the *above water mark*. For example, if owning costs you an extra $1000 a month, and the above-water mark is 15 years away, its $1000 x 12 x 15, for roughly $180,000 in savings.

This is just a rough number, however, because there are lots of moving parts to take into account. For example, rent will likely increase over this time as well, so even if you would save $1000 a month today to rent, you may only be saving $500 a month by year ten, and $200 a month by year fifteen, for an average monthly savings of about $600 per month. This means that you'd actually save $108,000 ($600 x 12 x 15) rather than $180,000 over the 15 years. On the other hand, if you took the money that you saved each month for the next 15 years by renting and put it into a modestly performing investment account returning 3%, you'd be much closer to the $180,000 amount because the interest earned would roughly offset any annual increases in rent.

Moreover, you may be able to buy again in a few years, taking advantage of both a lower mortgage payment and future appreciation – resulting in more long term savings. Of course, many of the variables that you must take into account are only educated guesses, including how much your home will appreciate or depreciate, how much rent will increase, and how much you could make investing the money. Nobody can say for sure.

But you can still get a *rough* estimate of the amount you would save by renting instead of owning. To get a firmer estimate, you should consult with an accountant or financial planner. Even this rough calculation though underscores an important point: if you spend the money that you'd save by letting go of your home, then it won't help you much in the long run. Having more money in your pocket now may certainly make life easier and, if you're struggling to survive, you may desperately need this money. But unless you invest the savings, you're not doing much to improve your financial future. So, if you decide to let go of your home, you should try to invest as much as possible of the money that you save from renting. If you do, you might build yourself a nest egg after all, or have a substantial sum for a down payment on a home in a few years (if you decide to take the plunge again).

The Cost of Defaulting

Even though you may save a significant amount of money by renting instead of owning, there are costs associated with defaulting. We've talked about a lot of them, including the cost of moving, damaged credit, and the risk of a deficiency judgment. There are also intangible costs that we haven't discussed, such as the emotional costs of leaving your home and your neighborhood.

The moving costs are the easiest to figure out and are likely to be minimal compared to the savings. If you do the move yourself, moving may cost less than $1000. It's harder, however, to put a value on damaged credit or on the risk of a deficiency judgment. The value of your credit score will depend on how much you need credit in the next few years. For example, if you need a credit line to run a sole proprietorship, then your credit score could be extremely valuable to you. On the other hand, if you're moving to Ecuador and will be living on a cash basis for the next several years, your credit score may be completely worthless. For most people who are somewhere in between, it's harder to say.

One thing to consider is that insurance companies use credit scores to price auto insurance policies. It's said that a low credit score can increase the cost of automobile insurance anywhere from 20-50%. Assuming you're paying the national average for insurance now, which is $1,736 a year, that's a cost of between $347 and $868 a year for a couple years until your credit score improves. That's not completely insignificant, but you may save more than that in a single month of not paying your mortgage. A low credit score may also cause your interest rate on your credit cards to go up for new purchases (but not existing balances). This won't matter if you don't carry a balance, but may matter if you need to use your card in an emergency. If that happens, you may spend a few hundred more a year in interest due to a low credit score.

Emergencies aside, however, if you don't need to purchase anything on your credit card for the next few years, a poor credit score may cost you nothing at all other than a possible increase in automobile insurance - and only then if you need a new policy or decide to adjust your current one.

In addition to the cost of a low credit score, if any, you face the risk of deficiency judgment in most states if you default. As we discussed, one way to place a monetary value on this risk is to take the risk of the deficiency judgment and multiply it times the amount of the possible judgment. For example, if the deficiency would be $100,000 and the risk is 5%, it's .05 x $100,000, the expected cost is $5,000. But the actual calculation that you need to make is more subjective. The question, using the same example, is: how much would you be willing to lose on your house to avoid a 5% chance of a $100,000 deficiency? In answering this question, you should remember that, if it comes to it, you may be able to discharge any deficiency judgment in bankruptcy or settle for a lesser amount.

If you really can't tolerate risk, you might say to yourself "I'd be willing to lose $40,000 on my house to avoid a 5% chance of a $100,000 deficiency." If you're comfortable with risk, on the other hand, you may not be willing to lose any more than $5,000. Only you can decide how much avoiding the risk of a deficiency judgment is worth to you. But using the formula, "I'd be willing to lose $X on my house to avoid an X% chance of a $X deficiency," may be helpful in making your decision more concrete and less likely to be based on generalized anxiety.

Once you have some concrete dollar value placed on avoiding the risk of deficiency (such as $40,000 in the above example) add a few thousand for the possible cost of increased interest rates for a few years and the increased cost of auto insurance combined. Again, if you are risk-averse, you might want to use high numbers for the cost of increased interest rates and auto insurance, and come with something like $4,000. Add the $40,000, $4,000, $1,000 for moving, and them some dollar amount for how much you're willing to pay extra to live in your house instead of a rental. The grand total is how much it would "cost" you to default — or, viewed in reverse, how much not defaulting is worth to you.

No one can do this calculation for you. Different people will come up with different numbers, even when faced with exactly the same circumstances and risk. For example, in contrast to the risk-averse person in the above example, who comes up with a cost of default of more than $45,000, a risk neutral person might come with a cost of only $10,000 in the same situation.

But, as you can see even without doing the actual calculation for yourself, the costs of default aren't insignificant—especially for risk-averse individuals who live in a state where their lender may pursue them for a deficiency judgment or those who really love their homes. For this reason, few people *intentionally* default on their mortgage unless they are more than 10% underwater. Intentionally defaulting may not begin to make sense for most people until they are 25% percent or more underwater.

But the percent where it makes sense to default will also vary according to the size of the loan, state law, and the person. If you owe $200,000 and your home is 25% underwater, for example, that's about $50,000. It may not be worth the hassles and risks of default if you live in Alabama, where your lender could more easily pursue you for deficiency judgment. On the other hand, if you owe $1 million and are 25% underwater, that's $250,000. It may very well be worth the hassles and risks to default then, especially if you live in Arizona where your lender generally cannot pursue you for a deficiency judgment on a purchase money mortgage. Once the percentage underwater approaches or exceeds 50%, default may become attractive, and sensible, for many people regardless of the state. But whether it's sensible and attractive to you, in your particular situation, is your call alone.

Summing it Up

Only you can decide what's best for you, and you should probably do so in consultation with a professional. But to summarize the discussion above:

It _probably_ does not make financial sense to default on your mortgage if:

1. You're less than 10% underwater; <u>or</u>

2. Your monthly cost of owning is less, or only slightly more, than renting; <u>and</u>

3. You don't need to move.

It also _probably_ does not make financial sense to default on your mortgage if:

1. You have a particular need for credit, such as if you run a sole proprietorship.

2. You personally feel that your house is worth what you pay.

3. You need to move to another city or state, but could rent your house out to adequately cover your monthly costs.

4. You know based upon facts and not just fear that you would lose your security clearance if you defaulted.

5. You're unemployed and you know based upon facts and not just fear that your credit score would likely affect your employability.

6. You live in a state where your lender could pursue you for a deficiency judgment and the risk that they might is not worth the savings of default to *you*.

It *may* make financial sense to default if:

1. You're more that 10% underwater; and

2. You're paying significantly more on a monthly basis that you would to rent a similar home; and

3. One or more of the following factors apply:

   a. You're struggling to make ends meet;

   b. You're using credit cards to stay afloat;

   c. You're dipping into your savings or retirement to make your mortgage payment;

d. You're pouring your disposable income into your house and are not able to save for the future;

e. You need to move for a new job or some other compelling reason;

f. You live in a state and/or have a type of loan such that you're not at risk for a deficiency judgment; or

g. You would save a significant amount of money by defaulting and decide it's worth whatever costs and risks you may face.

Chapter 4: Weighing your Options

If you've done the above calculations, you now have a sense of how long it will be before you're no longer underwater and a rough number reflecting how much money you would save if you could get out from under your mortgage. You also now have an actual number representing the costs of default. This information may be sobering, or welcomed, depending on whether things are better or worse than you thought. If the information is sobering, it may be even clearer now than ever how much your mortgage is threatening your financial well-being. The next question is: what can you do about it?

Short-Sale

One attractive option, if your lender will agree, is a short-sale. A short-sale is when you sell your house for less than you owe on your mortgage(s). In other words, you sell "short" of your pay-off. Ideally, when you do a short-sale, your lender agrees to accept whatever the house sells for and to forgive the rest of your debt. A successful short-sale can have many benefits and lenders have grown more willing to agree to short-sales over time. One benefit is that you'll take less of a credit hit than with a foreclosure (though maybe only slightly less); and you're likely to be able to qualify to buy a new home in as little as two years. With a foreclosure, it can be as little as 3 years to as long as 7 years before you can do so. Most importantly, though, you can — and should — also negotiate with your lender to ensure that it releases you of any further liability as part of your agreeing to a short-sale, meaning that you would not face the risk of a deficiency judgment.

As such, a short-sale can be an excellent way out of an underwater home. Nevertheless, there are a few caveats. In order to agree to a short-sale, lenders generally expect a "seller contribution." This contribution can range anywhere from a few hundred to tens of thousands of dollars. A short-sale can also involve signing a "promissory note" for a portion of the unpaid primary mortgage. How much seller contribution the lender expects will depend on several factors, including how much it thinks that you can pay. This is why the lender will typically require you to document your income and assets before it agrees to a short-sale. Its goal is to squeeze as much money out of you as it can. Having your financial documents gives it information, leverage and power in figuring out how much it can make you pay before you squeal. If you have a lot of assets, or money in savings or investment accounts, a short-sale may be a costly option.

The lender's leverage and how much it will require as a seller contribution will also depend on whether it can theoretically pursue you for a deficiency judgment in your state, and how much it can scare you into thinking that it may actually pursue you.

How much the lender will demand will also depend on whether you're current on your mortgage or have stopped making payments. If you're current, your lender will assume that you care a lot about your credit score and that you'd be willing to pay a substantial amount to avoid damaging it. Also, the lender may figure that, if it doesn't agree to the short-sale, you'll go right on paying the mortgage. As discussed before, if that's the case, why should the lender take any loss?

If you have defaulted on your mortgage, however, the lender's only option other than a short-sale is to foreclose, or to accept a deed-in-lieu of foreclosure. Because both of these options may cost the lender more money than the short-sale, it may agree to the short-sale and ask for a small seller contribution, or no seller contribution at all. It may not like it, but it may not have a better option. Because of this, sometimes lenders will even pay homeowners to agree to the short-sale. Remember, it's all about leverage; and if you're still paying your mortgage, you'll have very little. That doesn't mean a short-sale is impossible; only that if you're still paying your mortgage, short-sales are usually harder to secure and will likely be more costly to you.

The last thing that you want to do is to make the short-sale harder, as there are already plenty of obstacles. First, they can sometimes take a long time to get approved, with stories of sellers waiting 6 months for an answer not unusual:

> Meanwhile, six months later, my agent was still unsuccessful in getting Countrywide to move off first base with a short-sale, and he walked away from the matter. I allowed the home to go into foreclosure at that point since I could not do a deed in lieu to

Countrywide because of the second mortgage on the house. – R. D.

We tried to short-sale our house and had 2 offers at the amount the mortgage company wanted. After 6 months of waiting for their approval, they sold our loan to an even more terrible company. Needless to say we have walked away from the house and are now renting one. We tried to save our house and our credit since Aug 2008, but like you already know, the mortgage companies have other agendas. – S. S.

Even if you don't give up, many buyers will, and you'll have to start over. If the buyer waits around, the answer after many months is still often no. And because short-sales take a long time to complete, you may not have time to complete one before the house is foreclosed upon. You should thus put your house on the market as a short-sale as soon as, or even before, you first default on your mortgage.

Second, if there's an additional loan on the property (such as a HELOC) both the first and any additional lenders must agree to the short-sale. Because a short-sale means that there will be little or nothing left for the additional lenders, they frequently don't agree. Indeed, if you have one or more loans on your house in addition to your primary mortgage, you should approach a short-sale with realistically low expectations. It may work out, but there's probably a better chance that it won't.

You should also understand going into the short-sale that the second lender, usually on a HELOC, isn't likely to waive or forgive the entire loan. It sometimes happens, but it's not common. That's because the sales price often won't even cover the first mortgage, much less the HELOC. Any additional lenders will want something, and they'll want it from you. Typically they'll want 10 - 30% of what is owed, in cash. They don't often offer promissory notes on these deals, either. They already have one — the HELOC. Now they'll want some cash. If you aren't willing to contribute some cash on any second and third loans, then you probably shouldn't bother trying a short-sale. The only exception is if you're completely insolvent and have no assets or savings (in which case the lender may agree because it has no other option). If that is your financial situation and you have other significant debts, you may want to consider bankruptcy.

Additionally, if you've pulled out a bunch of money from your house and spent it on things other than improving your house, and now expect the bank to completely forgive the loan, then you're probably not a good candidate for a short-sale. As we discussed above, you should think of the HELOC as similar to a credit card bill, not a mortgage. Credit card companies will sometimes accept less than is owed, but they always want something. The only real difference with a HELOC is that unlike your credit card company, your HELOC lender can theoretically come after your house. But if your house is underwater, it won't because it wouldn't do it any good to foreclose. All or most of the money from the foreclosure sale would probably go to pay the holder of the primary mortgage.

Third, if you're going to do a short-sale, know that it can be a hassle. Short-sales involve not only listing your house and keeping it ready for showings as with any listing, but also assembling a short-sale file, which can take many hours and requires detailed documentation. Then, if the approval process drags on, you can expect the lender to "lose" your file and/or demand updated information.

Fourth, a short-sale means making your situation highly visible, because you'll have to list your house on the Multiple Listing Service as a short-sale and usually put a sign in your yard. This visibility is in contrast to a foreclosure, which your neighbors may not learn about until you have already moved away.

These caveats aside, a short-sale can be a great way to shed your underwater mortgage. You may be a good candidate for a short-sale if you can show substantial hardship and have only one mortgage on your property. For the purposes of a short-sale, substantial hardship can include:

- Job loss
- Curtailment of income
- Divorce
- Addition to family
- Death or sickness in family
- Forced job transfer
- Deployment (military)
- Inability to work

- ARM adjustment (has to have happened, not 'going to' happen)
- Excessive debt

In addition, you need to be in default on your mortgage, or about to default, and you need to have some time before your home is scheduled for foreclosure. If you have a second or third loan on the house, you need to be prepared to make a substantial seller contribution.

If you think a short-sale may be for you, it's worth having a conversation with someone with experience in the process. A qualified short-sale agent can make all the difference in ensuring that you don't get tripped up by the issues discussed above. But there are a lot of real estate agents out there who claim to be experts on short-sales who aren't. Make sure that any agent you use can document their expertise and show proof that they successfully close a high percentage of their short-sales. And make sure they don't charge anything up front. Finally, if they suggest that it's immoral or otherwise wrong for you to default on your mortgage, find another agent. You want someone who will help you without judgment and who's clearly on your side.

Qualified real estate agents who help their clients navigate the process of completing a short-sale provide an extremely valuable service. But there are things that you need to understand about your real estate agent. First, your short-sale agent's primary job is closing the sale, not protecting you from your lender. Your lender will send a long list of financial information to your short-sale agent that it wants from you. Your agent will tell you that you need to provide all the information and that your lender will not approve the sale unless you do. Your agent may be adamant about this. That's what your agent was told by the lender and this may also be true based upon your agent's experience with other short-sales. Your agent may really want you to provide this information, because he or she may really want to close the deal.

Your agent may tell you that it's in your best interest to provide the information and your agent may indeed believe this to be true. But sometimes short-sales do close even when the borrower does not give the lender every piece of financial information that it wants, especially in non-recourse states like Arizona and California. This is because it doesn't matter what your financial situation is if your loan is non-recourse under state law. Your lender is entitled only to the house. You could be a billionaire and your lender can still only have the house and nothing else. Lenders get this, or at least can get it if you persistently explain it to them, and will *sometimes* relent and agree to a short-sale without all of your financial information.

Your short-sale agent may resist this approach, because he or she may be convinced that it will decrease the chance that the sale will go through. Your agent may be right. The problem is that if your agent is focusing on closing the deal, they may not have your future legal and financial protection in mind. Whether you disclose all your financial information or not, there is probably less than a 50-50 chance that the short-sale will be approved. This is true even if you can show substantial hardship, because strong incentives can drive lenders and loan servicers to prefer foreclosures to short-sales. For loan servicers, these incentives include the opportunity to make large fees off the foreclosure.

For lenders, the incentives to choose foreclosure over a short-sale include the possibility of collecting on the mortgage insurance policy; and the fact that the lender may not have to immediately reflect losses on its financial balance sheets from foreclosures, as it must do for short-sales. As long as it holds on to the house, the lender may be able to reflect it on their books at an inflated value. So sometimes banks decide it's better for them to foreclose and pretend on their books that the house is worth more than it really is. This is called "extend and pretend," which means extending the day of reckoning and pretending that everything is okay until then. A lot of this has been going on in the wake of the housing meltdown.

More critically for your purposes, if you have assets and a solid income that would allow you to pay your mortgage, there's little chance that your lender will approve a short-sale without a substantial seller contribution. Unless you're willing to make a significant contribution, disclosing your financial situation carries little benefit and significant risks. If your lender knows that you have money, it's more likely to pursue a deficiency judgment.

This is not to suggest that you hide your assets or that you misrepresent your situation, both of which you should not do. But you don't have an obligation to turn over all your financial information to your lender or answer any of their questions. This is critical to remember, because many homeowners report that their lenders have told them they have such an obligation. This is another reason to consider hiring an attorney, as then you can direct all your lenders calls to him or her.

Additionally, you should be aware that Fannie Mae has announced that it plans to direct servicers to identify people who default in the absence of substantial hardship so that it can pursue them for deficiency judgments and bar such individuals from getting another Fannie Mae-insured loan for 7 years. Fannie Mae's announcement may mostly be about scaring people, as it's almost impossible to identify a non-hardship default without detailed access to financial and other information about a borrower.

If you don't tell your lender, your lender isn't going to know what your personal situation is when you default and your file is less likely to raise any red flags. Instead, it will likely be processed along with the millions of other robo-foreclosures, which is exactly what you want if you're walking away. As such, unless you determine that you can show the kind of hardship that will convince your lender to agree to a short-sale, your best bet may be to remain silent. Your agent may not like it. They may even refuse to work with you. But for you, it's all about calculated risk and looking out for your own best interest. You must decide whether the chance of a short-sale is worth exposing the details of your financial life to your lender, who is, in some sense, your adversary.

On a related matter, if you have all your money with the same bank that holds your mortgage, then they already know your financial situation. But you might want to move at least some of your money elsewhere. It's just not a good idea to have all your money in a Bank of America account if you're about to default on a loan from Bank of America - or even if you don't plan on defaulting for that matter. They will, of course, know that you moved it. And it's illegal to act with the intent to hide your assets. But there's no reason to leave your money under your lender's nose, tempting them to take a bite. Indeed, if you do, some lenders *will* take a bite and just take the money for your mortgage payment right out of your account. The can do this if you have a Cross Collateralization Clause in your contract. To see if you do, you should consult with an attorney.

Voluntary Foreclosure

Another option is to just let your home go into foreclosure. We've already discussed in detail the benefits and consequences of foreclosure. If you need a refresher or skipped ahead to this point, it may be worthwhile to read the previous sections on "Anxiety about Foreclosure," "Fear of Being Pursued by Lender," "Concern for Credit Score", "The Costs of Doing Nothing" and "The Cost of Defaulting."

In short, the benefits of voluntary foreclosure may include shedding your toxic mortgage, saving thousands of dollars, and putting yourself back on the path to financial stability and security. The costs include damage to your credit score and a risk that your lender will pursue you for a deficiency judgment. In many cases, however, there is little to no risk of your lender pursuing you for a deficiency, and a temporarily damaged credit score shouldn't be a major concern for most individuals. Voluntary foreclosure is a business decision that you can make for yourself. It can thus be self-empowering. Your lender doesn't have to agree to voluntary foreclosure. It's the one option that's totally up to you.

What's not up to you is *when* your lender will foreclose. Your mortgage contract probably says that your lender can begin foreclosure as soon as 30 days after your first missed payment, but most lenders will wait at least 90 days. Many wait much longer. Lenders have more foreclosures than they can handle. If you're deeply underwater, they also really don't want your house. As such, there are cases where lenders don't even *start* foreclosing for a very long time, sometimes as long as 12 months.

The wait may be frustrating if you're anxious to move on with your life, but think of it as a free gift of time to live mortgage-free and save a lot of money. There's no need to feel guilty about this either. You're keeping the house from falling into disrepair. If you need to move, try to find a house sitter or rent the house on a month-to-month basis rather than just abandoning the property. You should also continue to pay any homeownership association dues. If you rent the house, you should probably let your lender know and set any rent in excess of homeownership association dues aside in case your lender ask for it, as your lender is legally entitled to do in most states. Check with an attorney to determine your precise obligations in your state.

Also, if you're really concerned about being fair to your lender, offer to move out immediately and send it the keys if it will accept a deed-in-lieu of foreclosure. It very likely won't accept your kind offer, but at least then you'll know that your lender has no one to blame but itself for your still being in the house. You'd gladly give your lender the house and move out; your lender just won't take it. If your lender accepts your offer, make sure that the deed-in-lieu is signed by your lender before you move and that they explicitly waive any right to pursue a deficiency judgment. A deed-in-lieu may result in slightly less of a hit to your credit score and your score can immediately start to recover; so it's a good option if your lender surprises you — and me — by accepting it.

Just as you shouldn't count on a deed-in-lieu, don't count on your lender being slow to foreclose. You should simply assume that you have the time allowed by law before you have to move. The clock does not start to tick, however, until your lender actually initiates foreclosure proceedings, at which point you'll receive an official foreclosure notice – typically called a "notice of trustee sale" or "notice of default." Don't be fooled by the "notices" that will arrive before the official notice in which your lender will threaten you with "imminent foreclosure." In some states (such as California) lenders have to send such notices before initiating foreclosure. In other states, they will send "imminent foreclosure" letters just to make sure that they're giving you proper notice.

The foreclosure process doesn't start though until they formally initiate foreclosure proceedings, at which point you'll receive formal legal notice, usually through certified mail and/or posting on your door. Most states also require the posting of foreclosure notices in local newspapers, though few people ever read or see them. You can see what kind of notice is required in your state by looking at the National Consumer Law Center survey on state foreclosure law (http://www.nclc.org/issues/state-foreclosure-laws.html).

The type of notice may be relevant to you if you remain concerned about what your friends, colleagues, or neighbors think. If you're really concerned about people knowing, you should be aware that, independent of any notice required by law, your house may also appear as a pre-foreclosure on websites like Zillow and Realty Trac, as those sites track and post that information. There could be other such sites as well.

After your lender begins the foreclosure process, how long it takes varies state-by-state. But your lender cannot foreclose faster than the law in your state allows. The amount of time to foreclosure can range from 15 days in Georgia (but then you have additional time before you need to move) to 12 months in some states. No matter what state you live in, you'll have some time to find a new place to live and prepare for the new stage in your life. You should, of course, consult with an attorney before you default to be sure how long.

Also, before you proceed to default, you should prepare mentally and practically for collection calls from your lender. One way to do this is to just cancel your phone and get a new cell phone. If you want to keep your landline, get caller ID and only answer if the call is from someone you know. If your lender's representative does happen to get you on the line, follow the example of others before you: politely tell the representative that you aren't going to be making any more payments, that the house is ready for foreclosure and to please get on with it. Tell the representative that you're hanging up and gently put down the phone. Your lender may keep calling, or they may get the message and leave you alone. If they call back, keep your cool, but be firm. Don't allow yourself to be bullied, threatened or shamed. They're in no place to judge you. This is your decision to make.

As previously discussed, being willing to accept foreclosure may also increase your chances of securing a loan modification or a short-sale. But you need to understand that if you default on your mortgage, foreclosure is the likely outcome. Even if you're defaulting in hopes of getting your lender to agree to a loan modification or to agree to a short-sale, it isn't required to do either. But since on balance you have a much better chance of getting a loan modification or completing a short-sale if you have stopped making payments, you may decide it's worth a calculated risk to default - even if you'd prefer to avoid foreclosure. But you have to be okay with giving up your house. If you've been anxious and stressed about being underwater for long enough, you may find foreclosure to be welcomed relief.

Bankruptcy

As previously discussed, bankruptcy may help protect you if you choose voluntary foreclosure and your lender decides to pursue you for a deficiency judgment. But bankruptcy may help in other ways as well.

First, if your house is currently a rental property, you may be able to have the mortgage principal reduced, or "crammed down," to the current fair market value of the house in Chapter 13 bankruptcy as part of a debt restructuring plan. Similarly, you may be able to have the interest rate reduced and the monthly payment adjusted so that it's covered by the rent your property generates. For example, if you owe $200,000 on your rental property but it is now worth only $130,000, you may be able to have the principal balance reduced by as much as $70,000. Similarly, if your monthly payment is currently $1,500, but you clear only $800 in rent, you may be able to have your monthly payment reduced. Whether this is an option for you will depend on your particular situation. But if you're underwater on a house that is now a rental property, then you probably owe it to yourself to consult with a bankruptcy attorney.

If your underwater home is currently your residence, your primary mortgage cannot be modified in bankruptcy. But HELOCs and other second and third mortgages can be modified in a Chapter 13 Bankruptcy if they are no longer actually secured by your house. This would be the case if you're underwater on your primary mortgage, but have a HELOC or other second mortgage on top of that. In bankruptcy, such unsecured second mortgages can be stripped from the house and reduced or eliminated altogether. This may help you avoid the need to default, allow you to keep your home, and help you get above water much quicker than you otherwise would – with the caveat that you will be required to live under a strict budget for 3 to 5 years.

It's helpful to take an example. Assume that Sam and Chris's house is now worth $200,000, but they have a primary first mortgage on which they still owe $210,000 and a HELOC on which they owe $90,000 – in which case they owe a total of $300,000 and are $100,000 underwater on their home. Because their primary mortgage exceeds the value of their house, the HELOC is no longer actually "secured" by their house. In other words, even if the HELOC lender foreclosed, there would be nothing left to pay the HELOC after paying the primary mortgage.

Because of this, Sam and Chris can have the HELOC "stripped" from their home in bankruptcy and turned into unsecured debt like credit card debt. Once it's reclassified, the debt can be immediately discharged in a Chapter 7 bankruptcy, or it can be folded into their overall debt repayment plan in a Chapter 13 bankruptcy. In Chapter 7, they may not have to pay any of the HELOC; whereas in Chapter 13, they will only have to pay a portion of it, with the remainder discharged at the end of their repayment plan. In Chapter 13, their repayment plan will either be three or five years, depending on their income. Either way, when they're done, the HELOC (as well as other second and third mortgages treated similarly) will be discharged. Moreover, their home may very well have appreciated enough in that time that they're no longer underwater on their primary mortgage. If so, they'll have positive equity in their home again. What's more, they'll still be in their house and their credit score will likely have recovered. That's not a bad outcome for a couple that was $100,000 underwater.

Before you decide to go this route, however, you should talk with a bankruptcy attorney. Indeed, this section is meant only to flag the issue for you: Chapter 13 bankruptcy *may* allow you to keep your house, get out from under any second or third mortgages, and help you reduce your other debt as well. It can be a way to be above water and back on your feet in just a few years. Whether you qualify for Chapter 13 bankruptcy depends on your debt levels, not your income. So if you are buried it debt, it may be more of an option for you than you think – though it has gotten somewhat more difficult to qualify for bankruptcy than it used to be and you need to be willing to live under a strict budget during the duration of the repayment plan. Talk to a bankruptcy attorney to see if bankruptcy might be available and helpful to you.

Finally, don't let the so-called "stigma" of bankruptcy hold you back. If you were a business, you'd consider bankruptcy. Indeed, US Airways, Chrysler, Sharper Image, the Disney Store, Delta Airlines, Kmart, Pacific Gas & Electric, Northwest Airlines, Conseco, American Standard, General Motors, Eddie Bauer, Crabtree & Evelyn, Samsonite,

Continental Airlines, and many other reputable companies have all filed for bankruptcy in the past. So you'd have plenty of company in using bankruptcy to get out of debt and back on your feet.

Loan Modification

Another option is to try to get a loan modification from your lender. For this, you're going to need some luck and a lot of perseverance. First, if you call your lender about a loan modification while you're current on your mortgage, your lender is probably not going to have any interest in talking to you. The simple reality is that lenders don't typically work with homeowners who are current on their payments. You may hear stories of lenders who have done so, but it's very rare.

You can, of course, call your lender yourself to find out. But be warned that it's in your lender's interest to keep you paying with the false hope of a loan modification. Though they would never admit it, this is why I think lenders will frequently invite homeowners to submit loan modification paperwork, even though the lender never intends to modify the loan. The longer your lender can keep you thinking that it may modify your loan and the longer you keep paying, the more money your lender makes. If, knowing this, you nevertheless decide to pursue a loan modification, be prepared for an immensely frustrating and ultimately unsuccessful process.

Moreover, you're very unlikely to get a loan modification unless your current mortgage payment exceeds 31% of your gross monthly income, which is your income before anything is taken out of your paycheck. This is because the federal government has limited participation in government-sponsored loan modification programs, such as Making Home

Affordable (HAMP), to individuals whose payments exceed this percentage. Moreover, government-sponsored programs are generally designed to bring the borrower's monthly payments down to this 31% threshold and no less.

This cut-off is purportedly based upon "the generally accepted definition of affordability," but, as you know, paying 31% of your gross income on a deeply underwater home, when you could rent the same home for much less, is by definition unaffordable. Paying 31% of your gross monthly income for a mortgage can also leave you with very little to spare, especially if you have other significant financial obligations, such as child care or medical bills. The 31% cut-off is also harsh if you are struggling to survive, but your payments don't quite exceed the 31% mark:

> Tried to get the Home Loan Mod done thru our lender to no avail. Our small income of $33,000 gross combined (I lost my $36,000 yr. sales job earlier this year to lay-off) means to our lender we can afford an $850 mortgage. So we don't qualify. The payment is $800. Doesn't matter that I have 3 children from a previous marriage I'm supporting. Doesn't matter that electric and gas prices are up. Nothing matters but the bottom line, 31%.-O.N.

Even leaving aside monthly budget concerns, 31%--or even 20%--of your income is a significant percentage. Once a home has become an albatross instead of an investment, struggling to pay a mortgage may make little financial sense if you could rent a similar home for less.

Another variant of the 31% problem is that if your lender doesn't think that 31% of your income is enough to make a modification economically worthwhile to it, then it isn't going to do the modification. Lenders aren't required to modify loans under any of the government programs. Their participation is voluntary, which means they're only going to modify your loan if they think that doing so will result in more income to them than foreclosing. It's just business to your lender.

A narrow exception to the 31% rule is the "Making Home Affordable Refinancing Program," which is supposed to allow underwater homeowners to refinance up to 125% of their home's current value at "today's lower interest rates," if they're current on their mortgage and their loan is held by Freddie Mac or Fannie Mae. Lender participation is voluntary in this as well, and most lenders haven't been interested in participating.

More critically, many underwater homeowners have loans that exceed 125% of their home's value and thus don't qualify. If you're underwater enough to be thinking about defaulting, there's a good chance you're one of them. Indeed, the 125% cut-off means that the very homeowners who are the most likely to be distraught about their situations are the least likely to get help. The most desperate underwater homeowners are simply left out in the cold, with no hope of refinancing:

I have also contacted Making Home Affordable and a counselor told me that as I am over 125% underwater due to severe decline in Los Angeles market, I am not eligible for any assistance and I should contact Chase directly, which I have already done and was refused. – N.Z

I've probably gone through the process of trying to refinance once every 6 months for the past 2 years, but have always been told my property doesn't appraise at a high enough value to qualify for any loan programs. - O.M.

I couldn't refinance because my loan balance exceeded the value of my house by more than 125%. - Q. T.

Stories like these are extremely common. Indeed, in Nevada, over half of homeowners are more than 25% underwater; approximately 30% are more than 25% underwater in Arizona and Florida; and approximately 20% are more than 25% underwater in California. All of them are out of luck. If you're one of them, you aren't going to be able to refinance, either. Your only hope of reducing your payment or principal is a loan modification. Unfortunately, the hope is dim.

Knowing this, if you still wish to proceed, you should be prepared for the fact that you'll likely have great difficulty reaching anyone to discuss your loan modification once you submit it:

> I submitted my first modification request/proposal (which included a principal reduction to the then-current local market value) in January, followed by an addendum to that request in February. I called...and called...and called, trying to follow up, all to no avail. I continued making my payments, on both loans through April, and submitted another package, all the while telling both lenders that, after the April payments, I would have no money left. I received no response at all until I became delinquent for the May payments. – N.T.

> I have tried to work with my lender (Citimortgage) to attempt to get a reduction in the interest rate, however they're impossible to get a hold of much less work with. - H. I.

Second, be prepared to submit a lot of paperwork, and for your paperwork to be "lost" repeatedly:

> After losing my job in Jan last year, I set up an appt and application with HOPE in late April - and have yet to receive a decision from Chase about my home

modification request. They've lost my info 5 times and are the most unprofessional, unqualified group I've had to deal with. -T.N.

After dealing with a balloon mortgage myself and having the bank "lose" my modification paperwork 3 times, I became wise to their game. -S.G.

Third, be prepared to be treated rudely and lied to:

I cannot count the number of times I have called BOA and been treated rudely, lied to, disconnected, sent to wrong extensions, etc... Consequently, you can imagine the frustration I am feeling. I rue the day I even considered modification. -M.C.

My loan servicer routinely, regularly and knowingly lied to me about the legal and tax consequences of my own default in their attempts to get me to pay in full in spite of being $800,000.00 upside down. -K.I.

Fourth, be prepared to be threatened:

All this time, I was trying to work with someone...anyone...to figure something out so I could stay in my house, however, it became painfully obvious to me that the lenders just weren't interested in working with me, other than to make threatening phone calls. – N.S.

Their collections department continues to threaten actions towards foreclosure despite the fact that I am told I am in the trial period. –T.L.

Fifth, be prepared to wait months for an answer:

I started their painful "process" on March 27, 2009. It's now February 2010 and we have still not received the help of a modification. – M.S.

Worse, after months of frustration, be prepared to learn that your lender isn't willing to work with you after all:

In summation, I began this process with the hope of being able to keep my home by lowering my monthly mortgage payment. At that time, I was told that the worst case scenario was that I would be rejected and would be in no worse financial standing than when I began the process. As it stands right now, eleven months later: I am listed as being delinquent on my mortgage; my credit history has been damaged; I have lost access to several thousand dollars in unsecured debt; none of my phone calls to Citimortgage attempting to resolve these issues has been returned; I have instead only received letters threatening acceleration and foreclosure; and now I have been supposedly rejected from HAMP based on grossly inaccurate information. – E.D.

I have been trying to work with my former servicer and most recently Bank of America (my mortgage servicer sold it to them last year) for almost two years now, ever since my husband lost his construction job in the very beginning of the recession. I was stonewalled by all the usual excuses you've heard (lost paperwork, wrong paperwork, not enough people, new rules, new programs etc. ad nauseum) and lied to, patronized, castigated, hung up on, transferred endlessly, shamed and ignored finally. - K. D.

Understand, as well, that if you're offered a loan modification, it may barely reduce your monthly payment and will frequently increase your negative equity:

I tried to get Citi to modify my loan due to unemployment, an interest only loan, and an upside down house to the tune of $300,000.00. After being lied to, manipulated, making trial payments that they said were the precursor to the permanent loan and then having them cancel that program, I managed to get them to lower our payment $160.00 per month. They tacked on $35,000.00 to the backend of the loan in the process. I did the math and it's gonna cost us another $175,000.00 in interest in addition to the previous debt (if we pay it off) to save $9,600.00 over ten years. –R. B.

Even if you're offered a financially meaningful "trial modification," be aware that your lender might report you as delinquent during the trial period, and the credit score you were trying to save will be damaged, anyway:

What many people don't know when they apply for this type of modification, is that the banks cash your mortgage checks and place these funds in a separate file. The monies are not applied to your account. Therefore, in the months that pass by, your account is reported as delinquent to the credit bureaus........an acquaintance learned the hard way. When I heard this information, I feared my credit would be ruined as well, and cancelled my modification request. – M. C.

If you nevertheless accept a trial modification, be prepared to get stuck in it for months with no indication from the lender as to when, if ever, it will become permanent:

> I have been waiting for a home modification to go through, and have made (13) Trial Payments since January of 09. During that timeframe, it has been as if my loan has been under a shroud of secrecy where I am totally at the mercy of the lender. The trial was supposed to only last three months, and, here I am, 13 months later, with what feels like "no end in sight". – N.H.

> I made my initial 3 trial payments last year, and was initially due to receive new loan docs by October 09. Well, here it's the end of January, and I am still making trial payments with still no assurance that my modification is going to go through. - I. H.

> I am now 10 months into a request for a loan modification under the President's "Making Homes Affordable" program and I fear that no matter what steps I take I will still lose my home and my ability to ever be out of debt. I have been paying my "Trial Payment" since August of 2009. - T. L.

Finally, you should be prepared to learn after months of waiting that the initial hope was false and that your permanent loan modification has been denied, even though you did everything you were asked to do. Your lender wants to get as much money out of you as it can, until it's ready to begin the foreclosure process. So it's in the interest of the lender to make you think you'll get a loan modification right up until the point that it decides to pull the rug out from under your feet.

The simple fact is that most trial modifications never do become permanent. So far, the federal program known as Making Home Affordable, has helped only about 200,000 borrowers get a permanent loan modification; compared to 16 million who are underwater and more than 6.5 million who have lost or given up their homes to foreclosure. According to some estimates, less than 2 percent of loan modification applications actually succeed.

Of course, you may be one of the lucky ones. Every loan modification company posts testimonials and happy pictures online of their satisfied customers who get great loan modifications. I'd be smiling too if I won the lottery. But the reality is that you're not likely to get a loan modification; and, to have any hope, you have to fit a particular profile. As an initial matter, you're very unlikely to qualify for a loan modification if your mortgage payment does not exceed 31% of your gross monthly income.

Additionally, even if you meet the above 31% of your gross monthly income threshold, you're going to have to demonstrate substantial hardship. Substantial hardships include unemployment, significant loss of income, serious illness, and sometimes divorce or having to relocate. If you can't show substantial hardship, as your lender defines the term, it will probably snow in Miami before you get a loan modification.

Even if you can demonstrate substantial hardship, you'll also need to demonstrate that you have a steady source of income, and could make the payment if it was lower. In other words, you have to be facing a substantial hardship, but not too much hardship that you can't make whatever the lender considers is a reasonable modified mortgage payment. It's not easy to thread the needle in order to qualify.

If you're unemployed through no fault of your own, you probably feel this means that your lender should give you a break. Most compassionate people would likely agree. But your lender sees your being unemployed as evidence that a loan modification isn't going to do it any good because you still couldn't make the payment. As discussed, your lender is a corporation that doesn't feel empathy. It modifies mortgages only when profitable to do so.

Finally, even if you can demonstrate substantial hardship, even if you can prove that you could make a lower payment, and even if you jump through every hoop they ask you to jump through, the unfortunate reality is that you still aren't likely to get a loan modification. You also aren't likely to learn this bad news for a very long time, and until you have dumped thousands more dollars into your underwater home.

I don't tell you all this or share the stories of others just to discourage you. Rather, before getting your hopes up, it's important to hear from others the emotional impact of being flatly refused help, or learning, after months of waiting, that the initial hope was false. It's enough to push many underwater homeowners from a state of anxiety to a state of despair. The cruel reality is that you aren't likely to get a loan modification. Better to learn this now than after you've invested a year into the process.

Knowing what likely lies ahead, you should think carefully whether you want to put yourself or your family through the process of trying to get a loan modification. And remember that if your net monthly owning costs are more than what you would pay for rent, you're losing money every month that you keep making your mortgage payment. Finally, don't ever pay someone up-front who promises to get you a loan modification. You'll be wasting your money.

On the other hand, you need an advocate on your side. The loan modification process is complex and mystifying and banks are recalcitrant. So, if you're determined to press on with a loan modification, you should hire a loan modification company that will represent you for no upfront fee or contact a housing counseling agency, which will assist you free of charge. Because housing counseling agencies generally have relationships with lenders, they have as good a chance as anyone of helping you make a loan modification happen.

Buying and Bailing

One of the most controversial practices related to mortgage default is called "Buy and Bail." This is when a borrower buys a new house, usually with a new mortgage, while their credit's still intact and then bails on their old mortgage. The great advantage of "buying and bailing" is that one has a new home and is likely buying in at or near the bottom of the market. One who buys and bails thus has the potential to benefit from appreciation as the market recovers, instead of paying the mortgage on an overpriced house while waiting perhaps a decade or more just to be above water again.

Because this is such an attractive option for underwater homeowners, lenders want to do whatever they can to keep you from doing it. So, they have universally adopted a requirement that in order to qualify for a loan to buy a second home, you must be able to qualify for both your current and future home without including any potential rental income on either home. In other words, you have to be able to pay both mortgages at the same time on your current income alone. This puts the possibility of buying and bailing out of reach for most people. Those who have sufficient income may still have the option.

Aside from whether buying and bailing is a financially viable option, however, some have argued that it's fraud. To this I reply, fraud on who? Fraud is entering into a mortgage contract with the intent not to perform or giving false information to induce the lender to loan money. If the person buying and bailing intends to pay the mortgage on the second house and didn't present any false information (such as a fake rental agreement for their current house) then they're not defrauding the lender on the new mortgage. If they did not buy their first house with the prior intent to default, then they did not defraud that lender, either. Absent misrepresentation (such as signing a statement "verifying" that you don't intend to default on your other mortgage) the argument that buying and bailing is fraud seems to have little basis. The word fraud seems to be thrown around mostly to frighten people. Being accused of fraud is scary, so the use of the word itself helps deter people from buying and bailing.

Putting aside the suggestion that it constitutes fraud, buying and bailing does indicate that the individual doing it may have money to pay a deficiency judgment. As such, it's a risky strategy unless you live in an anti-deficiency state and have only a purchase money mortgage on your home. Your current lender(s) will know that you took out a new mortgage, as it will appear on your credit report. That doesn't mean your lender(s) would actually pursue a deficiency judgment against you, but it does increase the risk by some unquantifiable but significant amount. Only you can decide if it's worth the risk.

Choosing to Stay

A final option, of course, is to stick it out. As we discussed, this may be the wisest choice if you are less than 10% underwater *or* your net monthly cost of owning is less or slightly more than it would cost to rent a similar home. You've got to live somewhere. Living in your own home has advantages that are probably worth paying a little more for each month.

Indeed, if you've raised children in your home, lovingly made it just right for you, or are otherwise deeply attached to your home, it may be worth considerably more each month than you'd pay to rent a "comparable" house. If you really love your home, can afford your payment, and it's worth the costs to you, there's really no issue. You should stay. It doesn't matter whether it's a "rational" financial decision or not, whatever that's supposed to mean. If you love your house and don't want to move, that's a good enough reason to stay in an underwater home. Turn off the news, avoid distressing stories about the real estate market, and just enjoy your home.

The bigger issue is if you love your home but are struggling to make your mortgage payment. In such case, you have a few options. The first is to try to work out a loan modification. As discussed, you can't count on that. The better path may be to file for bankruptcy. Indeed, if you have already received a notice of default, you should consider immediately filing for bankruptcy, as the bankruptcy proceeding will require the lender to put the foreclosure on hold. With bankruptcy, you should be able to have other debts discharged or restructured in such a way that you'll be able to afford your mortgage payment. But if you hesitate, you may lose your chance to save your house. Now is not the time to delay.

Despite the possible benefits of bankruptcy, the financial industry successfully defeated efforts to allow bankruptcy judges to reduce your mortgage payment on your primary, or first, mortgage. It's one of the few debts that can't be restructured in bankruptcy. As discussed above in the section on bankruptcy, if your home is worth less than your primary mortgage, you may be able to have HELOCs and other secondary mortgages stripped, reduced, and ultimately discharged. This alone could save your home. But bankruptcy will only work if you could make your primary mortgage payment if your other debts were reduced. If your primary mortgage payment exceeds your income, even bankruptcy is not going to save your home.

In that case, you may try to fight the foreclosure in court. Most efforts to fight foreclosure are ultimately unsuccessful, but you may buy yourself some time. There are also some cases of homeowners who have been able to successfully fight foreclosure by showing that the lender cannot prove that they own the loan. Successful cases on this ground are traditionally very rare, but are becoming more common, especially in judicial foreclosure states. There's growing evidence that legal recording requirements were ignored when many mortgages were securitized and then sold and resold many times over. As a result, *some* judges have become more receptive to arguments that banks who claim the right to foreclose don't, in fact, have the documents required to show that they own the loans. In cases where courts order banks to produce the documents, many banks apparently cannot and thus cease the foreclosure process.

It's too early to tell how this will turn out, as the banks have been pressuring Congress to pass a law allowing them to foreclose without the traditionally required documents. In addition, many judges remain largely unsympathetic to homeowners who are in default. Judges thus not infrequently excuse the bank's errors and allow them to foreclose, anyway. My gut tells me that this issue will eventually be resolved in favor of the banks. There's already a lot of fear-mongering from Wall Street and in Washington about the economy getting worse if banks can't foreclose and investors take more losses as a result. If history is any guide, this threat will be enough for banks to get their way either in Congress or in the courts. I hope I'm wrong. And you can certainly try to fight foreclosure. But I wouldn't count on being successful, even if your bank didn't follow the rules. Nevertheless, you should contact an attorney immediately to discuss your options. There are also anti-foreclosure community groups that you might rally to your cause.

If you want to try to get a loan modification, you can contact a housing counseling agency, which may be able to help with your lender and will usually do so without charging you a fee. Again, don't delay, or it may be too late. Housing counseling agencies, which are typically funded by the government and the mortgage banking industry, are often good at helping people work to get loan modifications or forbearances. They also frequently have special relationships with lenders, so consider contacting a housing counseling agency if staying in your home is your goal.

Summary of Options

Only you can decide what is best for you and you should consult with a professional. But if you're underwater on your home, you have five basic options:

1. Loan Modification
2. Short-Sale
3. Voluntary Foreclosure (or Deed-in-Lieu of Foreclosure)
4. Bankruptcy
5. Stick it Out

A *loan modification* may make sense if:

1. You want to keep your house;

2. You can document both substantial hardship and that you would be able to make a modified payment;

3. You are already in default or can prove that you are facing imminent default; and

4. You have patience and perseverance.

A *short-sale* may make sense if:

1. You don't want to keep your house;

2. You can demonstrate hardship such as
    - Job loss
    - Curtailment of income
    - Divorce
    - Addition to family
    - Death or sickness in family
    - Forced job transfer
    - Deployment (military)
    - Inability to work
    - ARM adjustment (has to have happened, not 'going to' happen)
    - Excessive debt;

3. You're in default or are willing to default; and,

4. You're willing to make some type of seller contribution (the size of which will depend on whether you live in a recourse state or not and how much money you have in your bank account).

Voluntary Foreclosure may make sense if:

1. You're ready to give up your house;

2. You don't want to deal with the hassles of a short-sale;

3. You can live with limited credit for a while; and,

4. You live in a non-recourse state or have a loan such that there is no risk of a deficiency judgment; or

5. You live in a recourse state, but are willing to accept the risk of a deficiency judgment, with the back-up that you may be able to have it discharged in bankruptcy or negotiate a settlement.

You should consider *bankruptcy* if:

1. You'd like to keep your home;

2. You're underwater on your primarily (first) mortgage and also have a HELOC or other secondary home loan;

3. You're struggling to pay bills;

4. You have other debt that you'd also like to get under control;

5. You're willing to give up some assets under Chapter 7 bankruptcy or are willing to live under a debt restructuring and repayment plan under Chapter 13 bankruptcy for a 3-5 years; and,

6. The idea of being above-water and debt-free in a few years sounds attractive.

You should probably *stick it out* if:

1. You're less that 10% underwater;

2. You're not paying significantly more than you would to rent a similar home; or

3. You love your house.

Conclusion

Hope for the Future

After all the anxiety and stress of trying to figure out what to do, many underwater homeowners find a sense of empowerment and relief in letting go of their homes. As one homeowner explained, "Choosing to walk away was the hardest thing I think I've ever battled with. After walking away, I have felt nothing but relief." This relief is especially powerful to the extent that homeowners have already psychologically let go of their emotional attachment to their homes and feel trapped in a debtor's prison from which they'd like to escape. Like a person who finally leaves an unhealthy relationship after years of wanting to do so, many people who give up their homes report feeling free again and hopeful about the future.

Indeed, a toxic relationship or marriage is a good way to think about an underwater mortgage. When you signed your mortgage and got the keys to your new home, you knew you were making a big commitment, but it was one made full of hope and dreams for the future. The common understanding of you, the lender, your agent and everyone involved was that, though homeownership may have its challenges, it's ultimately one with great rewards. You didn't expect that the housing market would crash and that you'd end up in a toxic mortgage that keeps you awake at night worried, threatens your ability to retire or send your children to college, and generally makes you miserable with anxiety and regret.

Yes, you signed a contract with your mortgage company, but you can think of the contract as similar to a prenuptial agreement when getting married. Both parties hope things will work out and commit to try to make it work. But both also understand that it may not. As such, they agree in advance who gets what if they dissolve the relationship. Your agreement with your lender is that they get the house.

Additionally, in any relationship, both parties have an obligation to make compromises when unexpected circumstances make things difficult. When one party obstinately refuses to do so in a marriage, it's sometimes called a toxic marriage. Given the behavior of many mortgage companies, it's not surprising that one homeowner wrote to me describing her mortgage company as her "abusive husband." That may be a bit overstated, but it can feel a lot like that. You call your mortgage company to work things out and they blame you, make you feel guilty, and refuse to do anything on their part to make it better. They also threaten you if you suggest leaving the relationship and harass you with endless phone calls. If this were a marriage, you'd have grounds for an at-fault divorce. Why shouldn't you be able to leave your lender?

Over 96% of Americans think that it's acceptable to divorce in some circumstances, and over 62% think it's acceptable to divorce if it will simply make you happier. Yet, somehow, only 35% of Americans think it's *ever* acceptable to default on your mortgage, even if you're unemployed and *can't* pay your mortgage. A mortgage is more important than a marriage? That certainly can't be. But I've gotten calls from divorce mediators about clients who are walking out on their marriages, but think it's immoral to walk out on their mortgage. Ironically, sometimes being underwater and financially stressed are major contributors to their divorce in the first place. For some couples, breaking their mortgage contract could literally save their marriage contract.

Don't get me wrong. I think divorce is sometimes the best course of action. Sometimes things don't work out and it's better to part ways. No one should confine themselves to misery in a toxic relationship based upon some promise made in different times when both parties had different expectations for the future. But if this applies to a marriage, it applies in much greater force to a mortgage contract. Give yourself permission to let go. It's ok. You may finally find relief when you do.

Additional Information:

www.brentwhite.com

Academic Articles on the Housing Crisis by Brent White

Underwater and Not Walking Away: Shame, Fear and the Social Management of the Housing Crisis, WAKE FOREST LAW REView (2010)

Take this House and Shove it: The Emotional Drivers of Strategic Default, SMU LAW REVIEW (2010).

The Morality of Strategic Default, UCLA LAW REVIEW DISCOURSES (2010).

Trust, Expert Advice, and Realtor Responsibility in the Housing Meltdown, Arizona Legal Studies Discussion Paper (2010)

Articles by Professor White Available at:

www.brentwhite.com

Bibliography

Books, Journals, Academic Articles, and Reports

Manuel Adelino, Kristopher Gerardi & Paul S. Willen, *Why Don't Lenders Renegotiate More Home Mortgages? The Effect of Securitization* (Fed. Res. Bank of Atlanta, Working Paper No. 2009-17a, 2010)

Bradford P. Anderson, *Welcome to My Flipperhood: A Call To Repair the Residential Real Estate Tax Swindle*, 7 Geo. J.L. & Pub. Pol'y 415 (2009)

David Anderson & Sarah Hodges, *Credit Crisis Litigation: An Overview of Issues and Outcomes*, Banking & Fin. Serv. Pol'y Rep. (June 2009)

Damien Arthur & Pascale Quester, *Who's Afraid of That Ad? Applying Segmentation to the Protection Motivation Model*, 21 Psychol. & Marketing 671 (2004)

Robert B. Avery et al., *Credit Risk, Credit Scoring, and the Performance of Home Mortgages*, 82 Fed. Res. Bull. 621 (1996)

Patrick Bajari, Chenghuan Sean Chu & Minjung Park, *An Empirical Model of Subprime Mortgage Default From 2000 to 2007* (Nat'l Bureau of Econ. Research, Working Paper No. 14625, 2010)

Dean Baker, *Is the Housing Bubble Collapsing? 10 Economic Indicators to Watch*, Center for Economic and Policy Research, Issue Brief (June 2006)

Dean Baker & David Rosnik, *Will a Bursting Bubble Trouble Bernanke?: The Evidence for a Housing Bubble,* Center for Economic and Policy Research (Nov. 2005)

John A. Bargh & Tanya L. Chartrand, *The Unbearable Automaticity of Being*, 54 Am. Psychologist 462 (1999)

Oren Bar-Gill, *The Law, Economics and Psychology of Subprime Mortgage Contracts*, 94 Cornell L. Rev. 1073 (2009)

Oren Bar-Gill & Elizabeth Warren, *Making Credit Safer*, 157 U. Pa. L. Rev. (2008)

Andrew Benito & Haroon Mumtaz, *Consumption Excess Sensitivity, Liquidity Constraints and the Collateral Role of Housing* (Bank of Eng., Working Paper No. 306, 2008)

Neil Bhutta, Jane Dokko & Hui Shan, Fed. Reserve Bd., *The Depth of Negative Equity and Mortgage Default Decisions* (2010)

Lauren G. Block, *Self-Referenced Fear and Guilt Appeals: The Moderating Role of Self-Construal*, 35 J. Applied Soc. Psychol. 2290 (2005)

Jean Braucher, *Humpty Dumpty and the Foreclosure Crisis: Lessons from the Lackluster First Year of the Home Affordable Modification Program (HAMP)* (Ariz. Legal Studies, Discussion Paper No. 09-37, 2010)

Paul S. Calem et al., *Spatial Patterns of Mortgage Delinquency in Major U.S. Metropolitan Areas*, MarketPulse (June 2009)

Ken Chapman, *Fear Appeal Research: Perspective and Application*, 3 Am. Marketing Ass'n Summer Educator's Conf. Proc. 1 (1992)

Satyajit Chatterjee, Dean Corbae & José-Víctor Ríos-Rull, *A Theory of Credit Scoring and Competitive Pricing of Default Risk* (2007) (unpublished manuscript)

Ethan Cohen-Cole & Jonathan Morse, *Your House or Your Credit Card, Which Would You Choose? Personal Delinquency Tradeoffs and Precautionary Liquidity Motives* (University of Maryland & Fed. Res. Bank of Bos., Working Paper 2009)

Morris R. Cohen, *The Basis of Contract*, 46 Harv. L. Rev. 553 (1933)

Rebel A. Cole, *The Housing-Asset Relief Program: A Plan for Stabilizing the Housing and Securities Markets* (DePaul Univ. Dep'ts of Fin. & Real Estate, Working Paper, 2009)

Matthew Corder & Nyssa Roberts, *Understanding Dwellings Investment*, 48 Q. Bull. 393 (2008)

Yongheng Deng, John M. Quigley & Robert Van Order, *Mortgage Terminations, Heterogeneity and the Exercise of Mortgage Options*, 68 Econometrica 275 (2000)

Yongheng Deng & John M. Quigley, *Woodhead Behavior and the Pricing of Residential Mortgages* (Univ. of Cal., Berkeley Program on Hous. & Urban Policy Working Paper Series, Paper No. W00-004, 2004)

A. Mechele Dickerson, *The Myth of Home Ownership and Why Home Ownership Is Not Always a Good Thing*, 84 IND. L.J. 189 (2009)

Chris Dillow, *Housing Over-Confidence*, Investors Chron. (Apr. 27, 2009)

Richard Disney, Andrew Henley & David Jevons, *House Price Shocks, Negative Equity and Household Consumption in the UK in the 1990s* (Jan. 11, 2002) (unpublished manuscript)

Brett Dockwell Kravitz, Note, *Which Price Is Right? Valuing Real Estate Purchased in Bulk With Nonrecourse Promissory Notes: Epic Associates v. Commissioner*, 56 TAX LAW. 301 (2002)

Rashmi Dyal-Chand, *Human Worth as Collateral*, 38 Rutgers L.J. 793 (2007)

Alex Edmans, *The Responsible Homeowner Reward: An Incentive-Based Solution to Strategic Mortgage Default* (University of Pennsylvania, Wharton School of Business, 2010)

John Eekelaar, *Are Parents Morally Obliged to Care for Their Children?*, 11 O.J.L.S. 340 (1991)

Danielle Einstein & Kevin Lanning, *Shame, Guilt, Ego Development, and the Five-Factor Model of Personality*, 66 J. Personality 555 (1998)

Stephen Elias, THE FORECLOSURE SURVIVAL GUIDE: KEEP YOUR HOUSE OR WALK AWAY WITH MONEY IN YOUR POCKET, Nolo Press (2008)

Harold W. Elder et al., *Buyer Search Intensity and the Role of the Residential Real Estate Broker*, 18 J. Real Estate Fin. and Econ. 3 (May 1999)

Ralph D. Ellis & Natika Newton, *Introduction, in* CONSCIOUSNESS & EMOTION: AGENCY, CONSCIOUS CHOICE, AND SELECTIVE PERCEPTION (Ralph D. Ellis & Natika Newton eds., 2005)

Fernando V. Ferreira, Joseph Gyourko & Joseph Tracy, *Housing Busts and Household Mobility* (Nat'l Bureau of Econ. Research, Working Paper No. W14310, 2008)

Christopher L. Foote, Kristopher Gerardi & Paul S. Willen, *Negative Equity and Foreclosure: Theory and Evidence*, 64 J. of Urban Econ. 234 (2008)

Christopher L. Foote, Kristopher T. Gerardi, Lorenz Goette & Paul S. Willen, *Reducing Foreclosures* (Fed. Res. Bank of Bos., Pub. Policy Discussion Paper No. 09-2, 2009)

Christopher L. Foote et al., *A Proposal To Help Distressed Homeowners: A Government Payment-Sharing Plan* (Fed. Reserve Bank of Bos., Paper No. 09-1, 2009)

Charles Fried, CONTRACT AS PROMISE (1981)

Charles Fried, *Philosophy Matters*, 111 Harv. L. Rev. 1739 (1998)

Kelly Gallagher, *Rethinking the Fair Credit Reporting Act: When Requesting Credit Reports for "Employment Purposes" Goes Too Far*, 91 Iowa L. Rev. 1593 (July 2006)

Andra C. Ghent & Marianna Kudlyak, *Recourse and Residential Mortgage Default: Theory and Evidence from U.S. States* (Fed. Reserve Bank of Richmond, Working Paper No. 09-10, 2009)

C. Paige Goldman and Elizabeth Huntley, *What's the Scoop? Background Checks and the Fair Credit Reporting Act*, 71 Ala. Law. 146 (2010)

Laurie Goodman et al., *Housing Overhang/Shadow Inventory = Enormous Problem*, Amherst Mortgage Insight (2009)

Luigi Guiso, Paola Sapienza & Luigi Zingales, *Moral and Social Constraints to Strategic Default on Mortgages* (European Univ. Inst., Working Paper No. ECO 2009/27, 2009)

Russell Hardin, MORALITY WITHIN THE LIMITS OF REASON (1988).

Russell Hardin, TRUST AND TRUSTWORTHINESS (2004)

John P. Harding, Eric Rosenblatt & Vincent W. Yao, *The Contagion Effect of Foreclosed Properties*, 164 J. of Urban Econ. 164 (2008)

Tomas Hellebrandt, Sandhya Kawar & Matt Waldron, *The Economics and Estimation of Negative Equity*, 49 Q. Bull. 110 (2009)

Andrew Henley, *Residential Mobility, Housing Equity and the Labour Market*, 108 Econ. J. 414 (1998)

Carroll E. Izard, HUMAN EMOTIONS (1977)

Irving L. Janis & Seymour Feshbach, *Effects of Fear-Arousing Communications*, 48 J. Abnormal & Soc. Psychol. 78 (1953)

Dean Allen Kackley, Esq., THE LOAN MODIFICATION GUIDE: FOR HOMEOWNERS AND THEIR PROFESSIONAL ADVISORS (2009)

Michael S. Knoll, *Taxation, Negative Amortization and Affordable Mortgages*, 53 Ohio St. L.J. 1341 (1992)

157

Donald C. Lampe, Fred H. Miller & Alvin C. Harrell, *Introduction to the 2008 Annual Survey of Consumer Financial Services Law*, 63 Bus. Law. 561 (2008)

James E. Larsen et al., *The Ethics of Real Estate Agents: A Comparison of Realtor and Public Perceptions*, 10 J. Real Estate Prac. & Educ., no. 1 (2007)

Adam J. Levitin, *Resolving the Foreclosure Crisis: Modification of Mortgages in Bankruptcy* (2009)

Adam Levitin, *A Critique of the American Bankers Association's Study of Credit Card Regulation* (2009)

Adam J. Levitin & Joshua Goodman, *The Effect of Bankruptcy Strip-Down on Mortgage Markets* (2008)

Adam J. Levitin and Susan M. Wachter, *Explaining the Housing Bubble* (2010)

Deborah S. Levy & Christina Kwai-Choi Lee, *The Influence of Family Members on Housing Purchase Decisions*, 22 J. Prop. Investment & Fin. 4 (2004)

Francesco Mancini & Amelia Gangemi, *The Role of Responsibility and Fear of Guilt in Hypothesis-Testing*, 37 J. Behav. Therapy & Experimental Psychiatry 333 (2006)

Terry A. Maroney, *Emotional Competence, "Rational Understanding," and the Criminal Defendant*, 43 Am. Crim. L. Rev. 1375 (2006)

Christoph Merkle, *Emotion and Finance – An Interdisciplinary Approach to the Impact of Emotions on Financial Decision Making* (2007) (unpublished manuscript)

Dwight Merunka et al., *Modeling and Measuring the Impact of Fear, Guilt and Shame Appeals on Persuasion for Health Communication: A Study of Anti-Alcohol Messages Directed at Young Adults* (Euromed

Marseille Ecole De Management, Working Paper No. 04-2007, 2009)

P.C. Murray, *Real Estate Broker and the Buyer: Negligence and the Duty to Investigate*, 32 Vill. L. Rev. 939 (1987)

Grant S. Nelson, *Confronting the Mortgage Meltdown: A Brief for the Federalization of State Mortgage Foreclosure Law*, 37 Pepp. L. Rev. 583 (2010)

Michael J. O'Hara, *Governing for Genuine Profit*, 36 Vand. J. Transnat'l L. 765 (2003)

John O'Shaughnessy & Nicholas Jackson O'Shaughnessy, THE MARKETING POWER OF EMOTION (2003)

Kirsten A. Passyn & Mita Sujan, *Self-Accountability Emotions and Fear Appeals: Motivating Behavior*, 32 J. Consumer Res. 583 (2006)

Tomasz Piskorski, Amit Seru, and Vikrant Vig, *Securitization and Distressed Loan Renegotiation: Evidence from the Subprime Mortgage Crisis* (Chicago Booth School of Business Research Paper No. 09-02, 2010)

Eric A. Posner & Luigi Zingales, *The Housing Crisis and Bankruptcy Reform: The Prepackaged Chapter 13 Approach* (Booth Sch. of Bus., Univ. of Chi. Law & Econ., Olin Working Paper No. 459, 2009)

Roscoe Pound, *Liberty of Contract*, 18 Yale L.J. 454 (1909)

Hye Jin Rho, Danilo Pelletiere & Dean Baker, Ctr. for Econ. & Policy Research, *The Changing Prospects for Building Home Equity: An Updated Analysis of Rents and the Price of Housing in 100 Metropolitan Areas* (2008)

Mario J. Rizzo & Douglas Glen Whitman, *Little Brother Is Watching You: New Paternalism on the Slippery Slopes*, 51 Ariz. L. Rev 685 (2009)

Jennifer Robison & Hubble Smith, *Buying & Bailing: Walking Away from 'Underwater' Mortgage Has Pitfalls*, Las Vegas Rev.-J. (Aug. 30, 2009)

Josh Rosner, Graham Fisher, *Housing in the New Millennium: A Home Without Equity Is Just a Rental with Debt* (2001)

Lauren Ross, *The Internal Costs of Foreclosure: A Qualitative Study Exploring Issues of Trust, Insecurity, and Self in the Face of Foreclosure* (2009) (unpublished M.A. thesis, University of Delaware)

William Samuelson & Richard Zeckhauser, *Status Quo Bias in Decision Making*, 1 J. Risk & Uncertainty 7 (1988)

Paola Sapienza & Luigi Zingales, *The Results: Wave VI*, Financial Trust Index (Chicago Booth/Kellog School, Apr. 30, 2010)

Steven Shavell, *Is Breach of Contract Immoral?*, 56 Emory L.J. 439 (2006)

Margaret Hwang Smith & Gary Smith, *Bubble, Bubble, Where's the Housing Bubble?*, Brookings Papers on Econ. Activity (2006)

Susan J. Smith et al., *Performing (Housing) Markets*, 43 Urb. Stud. 81 (2006)

Janet A. Sniezek &Timothy Buckley, *Cueing and Cognitive Conflict in Judge-Advisor Decision Making*, 62 Org. Behav. & Hum. Decision Processes, no. 2 (1995)

R.H. Strotz, *Myopia and Inconsistency in Dynamic Utility Maximization*, 23 Rev. Econ. Stud. 165 (1956)

John R. Talbott, *Sell Now! The End of the Housing Bubble* (2006)

John R. Talbott, *The Coming Crash in the Housing Market: 10 Things You can Do Now to Protect Your Most Valuable Investment* (2003)

Lyn M. Van Swol & Janet A. Sniezek, *Factors Affecting the Acceptance of Expert Advice*, 44 British J. Soc. Psychol., no. 3 (2005)

Kerry D. Vandell, *Handing Over the Keys: A Perspective on Mortgage Default Research*, 21 J. Am. Real Est. & Urb. Econ. Ass'n 211 (1993)

K. Viswanath & David Demers, *Introduction: Mass Media from a Macrosocial Perspective*, *in* Mass Media, Social Control, and Social Change: A Macrosocial Perspective (David Demers & K. Viswanath eds., 1998)

Alan M. White, *Rewriting Contracts, Wholesale: Data on Voluntary Mortgage Modifications from 2007 and 2008 Remittance Reports*, 36 Fordham Urban L.J., 509 (2009)

Alan M. White, *Deleveraging the American Homeowner: The Failure of 2008 Voluntary Mortgage Contract Modifications*, 41 Conn. L. Rev. 1107 (2009)

Samuel Williston, *Freedom of Contract*, 6 Cornell L.Q. 365 (1921)

Alan Wolfe, *Whose Keeper? Social Science and Moral Obligation* (1989)

Lester C. Thurow, *Cash Versus In-Kind Transfers*, 64 Am. Econ. Rev. 190 (1974)

Susan E. Woodward, *A Study of Closing Costs for FHA Mortgages* (2008)

R.B. Zajonc, *Feeling and Thinking: Preferences Need No Inferences*, 35 Am. Psychologist 151 (1980)

Cong. Oversight Panel, *October Oversight Report: An Assessment of Foreclosure Mitigation Efforts After Six Months* (2009)

Deutsche Bank, *Drowning in Debt — A Look at "Underwater" Homeowners* (2009)

Deutsche Bank, *Update: The Outlook for U.S. Home Prices: Beyond the Bubble* (2009)

Experian & Oliver Wyman, *Experian-Oliver Wyman Market Intelligence Report: Understanding Strategic Default in Mortgages Part I* (2009)

First Am. CoreLogic, *Summary of Second Quarter 2009 Negative Equity Data from First American CoreLogic*, (2009)

First Am. CoreLogic, *First American CoreLogic Releases Q3 Negative Equity Data* (2009)

First Am. CoreLogic, *Underwater Mortgages on the Rise According to First American CoreLogic Q4 2009 Negative Equity Report Data* (2010)

John Rao, et., al., FORECLOSURES: DEFENSES, WORKOUTS, AND MORTGAGE SERVING, Third Edition (National Consumer Law Center 2010)

FRBSF Economic Letter, *House Prices and Fundamental Value*, 2004-27 (2004)

FYI Revisited: U.S. Home Prices: Does Bust Always Follow Boom? FDIC (2005)

House Prices and Consumer Spending, 46 Q. Bull. 142 (2006)

The Housing Bubble and Its Implications for the Economy Before the U.S. Senate Committee on Banking, Housing & Urban Affairs, XXXth Cong. (2006)

Memorandum for U.S. Dep't of Treasury on Making Home Affordable (2009)

Mortg. Bankers Ass'n, *National Delinquency Survey: Second Quarter 2009*

Mortg. Bankers Ass'n, *National Delinquency Survey: Third Quarter 2009*

Mortgage Forgiveness Debt Relief Act of 2007, Pub. L. No. 110-142, § 2, 121 Stat. 1803, 1803–04 (2007)

S&P/Case-Shiller Home Price Indices: Index Methodologies (March 2008)

Newspapers, Periodicals, and Online Resources

Edmund L. Andrews, *My Personal Credit Crisis*, N.Y. Times, May 14, 2009, (Magazine) at MM46

Curt Anderson, *Despite Foreclosure Halt, Mortgage Crisis Not Over*, Associated Press (Oct. 12, 2010)

Charles V. Bagli & Christine Haughney, *Wide Fallout in Failed Deal for Stuyvesant*, N.Y. Times (Jan. 26, 2010) at A1

Vikas Bajaj & Ron Nixon, *Subprime Loans Going from Boon to Housing Bane*, N. Y. Times (Dec. 6, 2006)

Vikas Bajaj, *Top Lender Sees Mortgage Woes for "Good" Risks*, N.Y. Times (July 25, 2007) at A1

Bruce Bartless, *Who Saw the Bubble Coming?*, Forbes (Jan. 2, 2009)

Peter C. Beller, *Why Housing Hasn't Bottomed*, Forbes.com (Oct. 15, 2009)

Katie Benner, *Don't Blame Bob Shiller for the Death of the Housing Market*, CNNMoney.com (July 7, 2009)

Kate Berry, *Wary of Default, Banks Curtail Loans to Investors*, Am. Banker, (Oct. 9, 2009)

Joseph Boven, *Fed's Mortgage Modification Program: Keep Your House, Lose Your Credit*, Colo. Indep. (April 8, 2010)

Michael J. Burry, Op-Ed., *I Saw the Crisis Coming, Why Didn't the Fed?*, N.Y. Times (Apr. 3, 2010) at WK10

Dean Calbreath, *Real Estate Cheerleader Concedes Price Drop*, S. D. Union Trib. (Apr. 15, 2007)

Sewell Chan, *Greenspan Concedes that the Fed Failed to Gauge the Bubble*, N.Y. Times (Mar. 18, 2010) at B1

Chris Dillow, *Housing Over-Confidence*, Investors Chron. (Apr. 27, 2009)

Brian Eckhouse, *Whether To Walk Away: Housing's Moral Minefield*, Las Vegas Sun (Mar. 22, 2009)

Richard Eskow, *Resident Evil: Are Struggling Homeowners as Immoral as the Big Banks?*, Huffington Post, (Apr. 1, 2010)

Lita Epstein, *20 Million Homeowners Project to be Underwater by 2011*, Housingwatch.com (Aug. 5, 2010)

Bill Falzett, *The Mortgage Crisis and the First Rule of the Con*, American Chronicle (Oct. 10, 2008)

G.M. Filisco, *Work Smart: Prsopecting Scripts*, Realtor® Magazine (Mar. 2008)

John D. Geanakoplos & Susan P. Koniak, Op-Ed., *Matters of Principal*, N.Y. Times (Mar. 5, 2009) at A31

Steven Gjerstad & Vernon L. Smith, Opinion, *From Bubble to Depression?*, Wall St. J. (Apr. 6, 2009)

Peter S. Goodman, *A Plan To Stem Foreclosures, Buried in a Paper Avalanche*, N.Y. Times (June 29, 2009) at A1

James Hagerty, *Reappraising Home Appraisers*, Wall St. J. (Aug. 18, 2009)

Kevin G. Hall, *Fixed-Rate Mortgage Foreclosures Rising: First-Quarter Numbers Offer Troubling Forecast*, Spokesman-Rev. (May 20, 2010)

Kenneth Harney, *The Nation's Housing: Walking Away from a Mortgage*, Wash. Post (Nov. 28, 2009) at E1.

Monica Hatcher, *Homeowners Walking Away from Underwater Mortgages*, Miami Herald (Oct. 24, 2009)

Alphonso Jackson, *Ask the White House* (Sept. 6, 2007)

Suzanne Kapner, *Setback for US Mortgage Sector*, Fin. Times (Apr. 30, 2010) (London)

Nancy Keates, *Realtors' Former Top Economist Says Don't Blame the Messenger*, Wall St. J., (Jan. 12, 2009) at A1

Marilyn Kennedy Melia, *Life After Foreclosure*, Bankrate.com (Sept. 4, 2009)

Barbara Kiviat, *Walking Away From Your Mortgage*, Time.com (June 19, 2008)

Paul Krugman, *How Did Economists Get It So Wrong?*, N.Y. Times (Sept. 6, 2009) at MM36

John Leland, *Facing Default, Some Abandon Homes to Banks*, N.Y. Times (Feb. 29, 2008) at A1

David Leonhardt, *Is Your House Overvalued?*, N.Y. Times (May 28, 2005) at C1

Dan Levy, *Morgan Stanley to Give Up 5 San Francisco Towers Bought at Peak*, Bloomberg (Dec. 17, 2009)

Francesca Levy, *Where Home Prices Are Hitting Bottom*, Forbes.com (Sept. 18, 2009)

Roger Lowenstein, *The Way We Live Now: Walk Away from Your Mortgage!*, N.Y. Times (Jan. 10, 2010) at MM15

Renae Merle, *Geithner Vows Crackdown on Lenders*, Wash. Post (Apr. 30, 2010) at A17

Luke Mullins, *12 Hidden Costs of Homeownership*, U.S. News & World Rep. (Apr. 8, 2010)

Shahien Nasiripour, *Don't Look Back: Major Players Continue To 'Walk Away' from Poor Mortgages*, Huffington Post (Jan. 25, 2010)

Shahien Nasiripour, *JPMorgan Chase Argues Against Mortgage Modifications, Citing Sanctity of Contracts*, Huffington Post (Apr. 12, 2010)

President Barack Obama, *Remarks by the President on the Housing Mortgage Crisis at Dobson High School* (Feb. 18, 2009).

Eric Posner & Luigi Zingales, *The Better, Cheaper Mortgage Fix*, Slate (Mar. 2, 2009)

Joe Rauch, *Wall St. Pins Foreclosure Fiasco on Homeowners*, MSNBC.COM, (Oct. 14, 2010)

Ralph Roberts, *Top Myths About Loan Modification*, Realty Times (Jan. 26, 2009)

Donna Rosato, *Confessions of a Former Real Estate Bull*, CNN.com (Jan. 6, 2009)

Nouriel Roubini, *The Biggest Slump in US Housing in the Last 40 Years"...or 53 Years?*, Roubini Global Economics (Aug. 23, 2006)

Timothy Schiller, *Housing: Boom or Bubble?* Federal Reserve Bank of Philadelphia Business Review (2006)

John A. Schoen, *Why It's a Bad Idea To Walk from the Mortgage*, MSNBC.com (Mar. 16, 2009)

Nelson D. Schwartz, *Mortgage Mess May Cost Big Banks Billions*, NY Times Online (Oct. 14, 2010)

David Streitfeld, *Feeling Misled on Home Price, Buyers Are Suing Their Agent*, N.Y. Times (Jan. 22, 2008) at A1

David Streitfeld, *They're Not Paying Anymore*, N.Y. Times (July 26, 2009) at WK6

David Streitfeld, *No Aid or Rebound in Sight, More Homeowners Just Walk Away*, N.Y. Times (Feb. 3, 2010) at A1

David Streitfeld, *Banks Resist Plans to Cut Mortgages*, N.Y. Times (Apr. 14, 2010) at B1

John B. Taylor, *How Government Created the Financial Crisis*, Wall St. J. (Feb. 9, 2009) at A19

Richard H. Thaler, *Underwater, but Will They Leave the Pool?*, N.Y. Times (Jan. 24, 2010) at BU3

Nick Timiraos, *Some Buy a New Home To Bail on the Old*, Wall St. J. (June 11, 2008) at A3

Peter Ubel, *Human Nature and the Financial Crisis*, Forbes (Feb. 22, 2009)

Louis Uchitelle, *Unsold Homes Tie Down Would-Be Transplants*, N.Y. Times (Apr. 3, 2008) at A1

Jim Wasserman, *Loan Modification Firms Banned from Demanding Upfront Fees*, Sacramento Bee (Oct. 13, 2009) at 6B

Lingling Wei, *Tishman Faces Office Downturn: Portfolio in Washington in Default; If No Risks, "Don't Have Any Rewards,"* Wall St. J. (Aug. 19, 2009) at C1

David Wessell, *When Home Values Don't Mesh*, Wall St. J. (Feb. 14, 2008) at A2

Liz Pulliam Weston, *Are You Foolish to Pay Your Mortgage?*, MSN Money (Dec. 9, 2009)

Liz Pulliam Weston, *When To Walk Away from a Mortgage*, MSN Money, (Nov. 18, 2009)

Robbie Whelan, *Foreclosure? Not so Fast*, Wall St. J. (Oct. 3, 2010)

Brent T. White & Luigi Zingales, *Is Strategic Default a Menace?*, City J. (Apr. 27, 2010)

Mark Whitehouse, *As Home Owners Face Strains, Market Bets on Loan Defaults*, Wall St. J. (Oct. 30, 2006) at A1

Mark Whitehouse, *American Dream 2: Default, Then Rent*, Wall St. J. (Dec. 16, 2009) at A1

Adam Zibel, *Banking Execs Skeptical on Mortgage Reductions*, Associated Press (Apr. 13, 2010)

Luigi Zingales, *The Menace of Strategic Default*, 20(2) City J. 47–51 (Spring 2010)

2010 Predictions from Shiller, Blinder, Rajan and More, Wall St. J. (Jan. 5, 2010)

Mortgage Defaults in America: Can Pay, Won't Pay, Economist (June 25, 2009)

NAR's Ad Blitz Spawns Major Media Coverage, Realtor Magazine (Nov. 7, 2006)

Made in the USA
Lexington, KY
20 February 2011